Late Bloomer: On Writing Later in Life

Late Bloomer:
On Writing Later in Life

Naomi Beth Wakan

Wolsak and Wynn

Author's photograph: Elias Wakan, www.eliaswakan.com
Cover Image: Elias Wakan, www.eliaswakan.com
Cover design: Julie McNeill

The publishers gratefully acknowledge the support of the Canada Council for the Arts, the Ontario Arts Council and the Book Publishing Industry Development Program (BPIDP) for their financial assistance.

The Canada Council | Le Conseil des Arts
for the Arts | du Canada

ONTARIO ARTS COUNCIL
CONSEIL DES ARTS DE L'ONTARIO

Wolsak and Wynn Publishers Ltd
196 Spadina Avenue, Suite 303
Toronto, ON
Canada M5T 2C2
www.wolsakandwynn.ca

Canadian   Patrimoine
Heritage   canadien

Library and Archives Canada Cataloguing in Publication

Wakan, Naomi
Late bloomer : on writing later in life / Naomi Beth Wakan.

Includes bibliographical references.
ISBN 1-894987-11-X

1. Authorship. 2. Older authors. I. Title.

PN153.W35 2006   808'.020846   C2006-904063-X
Printed in Canada

To Wolsak and Wynn, my publishers, for trusting their instincts and launching and supporting so many poets, particularly older ones.

"I have no patience with people who grow old at 60 just because they are entitled to a bus pass."
— Mary Wesley

"Writing is finally a series of permissions you give yourself to be expressive in certain ways. To leap.
To fly. To fall."
— Susan Sontag

"It's easy, after all, not to be a writer: most people aren't writers and very little harm comes to them."
— Julian Barnes

Introduction   9

Part 1

1. What are we waiting for?   13
    Yes it does exist – encountering ageism   23

2. Let's begin   26
    A room of one's own   26
    Capturing ideas and encouraging the muse   29
    On voice   35

3. What shall you write?   37
    You don't need a Wow! experience   37
    Finding your form   41
    Exploring my forms: poetry and essays   44
    On novels   50

4. Memoirs   53
    Kiss and tell   56

5. Frameworks and editing   62
    Something to hang your writing on   62
    On writer's block   65
    On editing in general   67
    Be gentle – reflections on editing poetry   69

6. Finding support and encouragement   76
    Workshops and classes   76
    Helping each other – support groups   79
    A little more on criticism and feedback   84

7. What to do when the work is finished   88
    Submission, and mainly rejection   93

Contents

Part 2 Interviews

8. The toll of years: an interview with myself   103

9. Mildred Tremblay   111

10. Jenni Gehlbach   118

11. Molly Ford   123

12. Murray Barbour   128

13. Winona Baker   131

14. Shirley Langer   137

15. Charles Roberts   143

16. Maralee Gerke   147

17. Adrienne Kemble   151

18. Jim Swift   156

19. Leanne McIntosh   161

20. John Nesling   166

21. Roy Innes   171

22. A final word   178

23. Web resources   179

24. Bibliography   180

Acknowledgements

I would like to acknowledge the wise and wonderful input to
Late Bloomer given by the people I interviewed in the latter part
of the book, particularly Jim Swift, who allowed me to 'over-edit'
his fine poem. Thanks also to all the folks who have attended my
Late Bloomers workshops – your feedback has been invaluable,
and to Noelle Allen, co-publisher at Wolsak and Wynn, who was
an encouraging and supportive editor who managed to bring out
the best in me. All my writing is assisted by the loving support
and eagle eye of my husband, Elias Wakan.

Haiku, permission granted by Ruth Yarrow

al-Ghuzzi's poem, "The Pen" permission granted by
Salma Khadra Jayyusi

Leanne McIntosh's poem, "Ground Hog Day" and
Mildred Tremblay's poem "Mothers" are published by
permission of Oolichan Books.

Murder in the Monashees (2005) by Roy Innes.
Reprinted by permission of NeWest Publishers Ltd.

Thanks also to Jenni Gehlbach, Molly Ford, Murray
Barbour, Winona Baker, Shirley Langer, Charles Roberts,
Maralee Gerke, Adrienne Kemble, Jim Swift, Leanne
McIntosh, Mildred Tremblay, Roy Innes and John Nesling
for the contribution of their writing.

Introduction

Although I have written poetry and articles sporadically since I was a young child, it was only in my 60s and 70s that I really found my own voice – and oddly enough the voice I found was that of the bouncy eight-year old who had started jotting down small verse in the first place.

My voice didn't come from a need to record my memoirs for posterity or, indeed, from the need to find that voice and get it out, but from the very practical problem of meeting a mortgage. So my writings at first simply paid bills. However, I was genuinely involved with the subjects I wrote about, whether it was the Japanese language, folk toys and stories from Japan, or the gathering and re-telling of folktales from all around the Pacific Rim.

Later, the need to talk from deeper within took over and I chose the forms of essay and poetry for this, particularly haiku. My book, *Haiku – one breath poetry,* had had the honour of being selected by the American Library Association and I felt comfortable using that form of poetry to start recording the small incidents of my life on the island of Gabriola, where I had quixotically chosen a home on which to start paying that mortgage.

As someone who has always supported others in their search for creative ways of expressing themselves, it is natural, as I age, that I look for ways of encouraging and supporting seniors who would like to start expressing themselves by writing. Therefore, I am addressing you Late Bloomers in this book – not because I am interested in you becoming famous writers, or even halfway-famous writers. Ambition can be a devastating impediment to getting your words down on paper, and is guaranteed to throw a thick pall over your own true voice. I'm writing this book to ask you a question. "Why not start writing now for the joy of it?" I'm hoping that you will.

PART 1

1What are we waiting for?

"I will write when – I retire, the mortgage is paid, the kids have left home, I have left home…" I have heard these excuses so many times, and said them a few times myself. As Cormac McCarthy said, "I never had any doubt about my abilities. I knew I could write. I just had to figure out how to eat while doing this." And, of course, though this is an honest reason to wait, it is still somewhat of a cop out.

Writers have written when pawning their last spare sweater for food, in bus stations (because they are homeless), with half a dozen kids swarming around, in war torn lands, while dying of cancer and even, in one amazing case, when fully paralysed except for the ability to move his left eye-lid… now what's your excuse? Now is the later you were waiting for.

The wish to write, or rather, to have written is strong. But then so is procrastination. How long can you put off starting to write, and aren't your excuses getting a little thin? The kids have left home, the mortgage is paid, the pensions have kicked in – what is left to do but write? Harlan Ellison admonishes, "If anyone can stop you from being a writer, then don't be one."

However, Harriet Doerr, herself a Late Bloomer, warns, "older people shouldn't take up serious writing as if it were a basket-weaving course." Having learned to make a good basket myself, I feel she is underestimating the difficulty of making one, however, her point is well taken. If you want to do more than happily get it all out on paper, that is, if you want to see yourself in print, reading some useful books for techniques, or taking a few classes might be advisable. I have listed some helpful books in the bibliography at the end of the book for those of you writing in earnest for the first time.

Harriet Doerr's warning reminds me of an alleged interchange between Margaret Atwood and a brain surgeon at a cocktail party. The brain surgeon was expounding on how, after he retired, he thought he might take up writing. Margaret Atwood tartly responded that when she retired, she would be thinking of brain surgery as a possible career change.

Writing often appears to be so much harder for writers than for other folks. I'm not sure why that is, all I know is that writing, as a career, does not give you the possible security, steady income, pension and health fund that say the life of a civil-servant would. Since I am addressing Late Bloomers, however, I am assuming, somewhat rashly perhaps, that such basic needs as hearth and health insurance have been taken care of by now.

Whether you have the health and financial stability to concentrate on your writing is for you to decide. If you do decide that now is the time, you may still need encouragement and empowerment before you begin. In Late Bloomer, I will add the voices of other writers to my own in order to provide you with just that. Here are some of them, providing you with some excellent reasons to start or, if you have already begun, to continue your writing.

"There are three reasons for becoming a writer; the first is that you need the money; the second that you have something to say that you think the world should know; the third that you can't think what to do with the long winter evenings." So states Quentin Crisp.

Alfred Kazin adds a few more psychologically-oriented reasons for writing. Please read himself/herself where Mr. Kazin has restricted it to himself. "In every real sense, the writer writes in order to teach himself, to understand himself, to satisfy himself; the publishing of his ideas is a curious anticlimax."

Leanne McIntosh, a very interesting BC poet, adds another even more therapeutic reason for writing. When she realized that she was too private a person, she began putting her writing out, which fulfilled two purposes – to share her being and to share her talent.

Well that lists eight reasons to write. To add a ninth, nowadays I write because there is nothing else I want to do more. I hope you feel that way too.

John Greenya commenting on a young writer said, 'He wanted to call himself a writer, but he didn't want to do the work.' Ah yes many of us want to have written a book, rather than to actually write a book. As even Carol Shields said, 'I find writing hard and what I love is having written rather than the actual writing.' But then she had actually written books.

Nancy Mairs says that, ''nothing thickens a writer's skin and strengthens her heart like the sudden vision of a new venture.'' I hope this new venture – you as writer – will thicken and strengthen you as much as you need.

Our fears and worries as we procrastinate become an unworkable list. Yet why not make a new list called "Reasons to Write," and put at the top of the list the 'sheer joy of expressing myself' and forget to enter any more. But for whatever reason you write, consider this quotation from Jorge Luis Borges: "When writers die they become books, which is, after all, not too bad an incarnation."

This book is for seniors like you, who have stood up, or stayed seated, but either way have lived. Now you're ready to write about it. But living doesn't stop as your first pension cheque arrives, and you start writing. Your writing will spur on your living. As Donald Murray says, "Writing is not apart from living. Writing is a kind of double living. The writer experiences everything twice: once in reality and once more in the mirror which waits always before and behind him."

Yet still we hesitate, maybe for fear that we will not be taken seriously. Or, on the other hand, for fear that we will be taken too seriously and promoted to heights far above, which might mean a serious change of our lifestyles.

Whether you want to get published or not, I have gathered below an inspiring group of seniors who started writing late in life and took off with great speed to make up for lost time. GrannyLit (and, I suppose GrandpaLit) is the new literary name for them. I am not writing about them to present the high goals of fame and fortune, but because each writer, in their own way, illustrates some aspect of writing that will encourage and advise Late Bloomers.

Norman Maclean began writing after he retired at the age of 73. His book, *A River Runs Through It,* was written in 1976 and won the 1977 Pulitzer Prize in Letters. He was encouraged to write by his children (as you probably are also) and *A River Runs Through It* is a semi-biographical account of his family. It was rejected by several trade publishers before being picked up by the university press where he had been an English professor, the University of Chicago. His line, "Eventually all things merge into one, and a river runs through it" is haunting; and running through the entire book is his fascination with fishing and, indeed, with water. If you have a strong drawing towards a particular interest, use it again and again in your writing; it is central to you and will be central in attracting people to your writing.

Then there's Laura Ingalls Wilder of *Little House on the Prairie* fame. Although she had written a column for a rural newspaper for some years, Laura didn't break into the big time until, encouraged and edited by her daughter Rose, at age 65 she started her Newberry Honor Award winning series for children. People debate whether Laura was an "untutored genius" and Rose just helped with encouragement and with her connections in the publishing world, or whether Rose actually shaped and rewrote her mother's manuscripts. Since Laura had been writing locally for years, I suspect the truth lies somewhere in between.

Laura said she wrote the stories of her childhood to help later generations of children understand how much America had changed during her lifetime. This is a good motive to get going on your memoirs, if memoirs are what you are thinking of beginning. These days, there are larger changes in technology and society in ten years than there were in fifty years in the previous century. Fads come in and fade out, countries break up and thousands of people become refugees in a flash. So the changes you have seen in your lifetime are important to note down to inform future generations.

Helen Hoover Santmyer wrote the 4 lb, 1,400 page *And Ladies of the Club* at age 84; a first book that spent 37 weeks on the New York Times best-seller list. She said, "I know that it's comforting to people that this has happened to me so late. If I have brought them hope, that is reason to be glad." A favourite quote of hers is, "Time – our youth – it never really goes, does it? It is all held in our minds." It is all there in our minds, just waiting for a lift to go down the mine shaft to retrieve.

Freddie Mae Baxter, the seventh of eight children, started to write about her own life at age 75 in *The Seventh Child: A Lucky Life* with the help of Gloria Bley Miller, a writer friend of Freddie's employer. Over a period of a year, Gloria taped Freddie's stories and then shaped them into what she thought was a good book, and Knopf agreed. It was Freddie's first book and received wonderful reviews.

Ms Baxter defines her ordinary life in this way: "I'm a somewhat everything and nothing big. I'm not stuck-up. I don't have none of that thinking that you're better than anybody. I haven't had anything big. I was just down-to-earth and I got along fine. I'm my own person, that's what it is and I'm still moving." Well, there's lots to be learned here for budding writers besides telling your stories onto tape or a CD. Freddie is telling you not to fret that you have had an ordinary life; it is whether you are your own person, or not, that is really the key to autobiography (and to poetry). And yes, don't forget, as Ms Baxter recommends, keep moving!

Jessie Lee Brown Foveaux sat down every day at the kitchen table and at 98 wrote a book of memoirs, later to be called *Any Given Day: The Life and Times of Jessie Lee Brown Foveaux: A Memoir of Twentieth Century America.* It was written to share with her family and friends. She was taking a program on memoir writing at a Senior's Centre and was fulfilling the exercises given by her teacher. When she was finished, she printed 30 copies for family and friends. Warner Books bought it for a million dollars! It was described as a perfectly ordinary life – the raising of eight children, a problem husband, the Depression – her hardships and triumphs. Why was it so successful? I think John Braine explains why beautifully when he says that, "if you are to be heard out of all those voices, if your name is going to mean something out of all those thousands of names, it will only be because you've presented your own experience truthfully."

Harriet Doerr (the lady who compared writing to basket-weaving) finished her degree at 67 (she had started it in 1930), and at 73 wrote her first novel, *Stones of Ibarra,* a National and American Book Award Winner. She wrote it from her accumulated years spent in Mexico with her husband. Later in life, she was legally blind and when her publisher suggested she dictate further books to a secretary, she demurred saying, "I operate from chaos and have all sorts of secret approaches to my work. I don't think I could do it with an audience...other people don't need to be alone with their thoughts so much. I sort of starve if I don't have time alone." Do you also need time alone? Sometimes we writers fill our lives with activities, and clutter them with people as yet one more excuse for not writing.

Sheila Quigley was seven before she started to teach herself to read. She left school at fifteen and became a presser in a tailoring factory. She was married at eighteen and at 55 signed a deal for £300,000 for a thriller with Random House (this was for a two-book deal). Her story goes like this: After numerous rejections of earlier writing, she submitted a screenplay to an agent. He found it rough and gritty but recognised that here was real story-telling talent. He asked her to write a gangster novel set in northeast England. She was thrilled. "If he had said would I write a book about Martians set in the Northeast, would you write a cricket book, anything, I would have given it a go," she said. Her submission for *Run for Home* was guided through numerous rewrites by a supportive agent, who went on to get her a great deal. Getting a good agent is almost as difficult as getting a good publisher, but in Ms Quigly's case she got both!

Mary Wesley wrote her first adult novel, *Jumping the Queue,* (at near 70) becoming unexpectedly famous, and at 72 became a commercial success with her novel *Camomile Lawn.* She used gutsy heroines and wrote about women in a fresh new way. She approached sex directly in her writings saying, "The idea that people go on being sexy all their lives is little explored in fiction. The young always like to think they invented sex and somehow hold full literary rights on the subject." Her fondness for the West Country and her memories of Devon have formed the background for many of her books. The idea of using a sense of place, a particular area of which you have memories, gives a strong setting for any kind of writing you might like to hang on it. I used a small provincial park near where I live for *Drumbeg Park,* a focus for my favourite forms of writing – essay and haiku.

Brenda Rickman, a retired Tennessee school librarian, wrote *The Illuminator,* her first novel, when she was 60. It was translated into 10 languages and became an American Library Association selection. Ms Rickman says, "Pursuing a dream keeps you young. But whatever goal you have, being older gets you there faster because you have a sense of urgency."

She points out the importance of the fact that she had little successes on the way, the odd piece getting printed in a magazine or newspaper at just the right moment, perhaps when she was beginning to think her novel would never get finished. So if you are starting a lengthy memoir, or novel, remember to pause and submit smaller pieces, for their acceptance will sustain you in your efforts.

As I said before, it's not the fact that all these authors won fame and fortune that is important, but that they all took risks and wrote books, some of them lengthy, in their later years. They showed great persistence and proved that age was no limitation. As Mary Wesley so aptly said, "I have no patience with people who grow old at 60 just because they are entitled to a bus pass. 60 should be the time to start something new, not to put your feet up."

Yes it does exist – encountering ageism

Now that we have declared age is no excuse for not writing, let's look a little at ageism. Ageism is a definite presence that might delay, or even prevent, those of you who wish to publish your work from getting it out there.

Recently I helped organize a poetry festival on the small island where I live. When I suggested using the Seniors Recreation Centre as a venue, one of the helpers remarked, "Oh no! We couldn't hold it there. That's for old people!" As if old people couldn't write perfectly good poetry and appreciate poetry as much as the younger crowd.

Ageism doesn't count so much in the creative process, I think, but when it comes to marketing your work it is a different matter. As a TV writer, Burt Prelusky, put it rather crudely, "Too old to be hired, too young to be buried." In fact in 2000, Hollywood's older writers sued TV networks, talent agencies and entertainment companies claiming discrimination on the basis of age.

Checking with older writers whom I know, the advice is still to leave out information that could lead to the editor guessing your age when you submit your manuscript. Often this is not possible, so you are taking a chance, but if the submission is strong enough and catches the publisher's eye,

I can assure you your age won't matter a jot. Moreover, if you can also persuade the publisher that there is a target audience for your book/article/poetry and that there is little published on your subject out there, then the question of your age will completely disappear from the agenda.

Agents, however, have a different view about accepting an older client for two reasons. Firstly, if they have to choose between two equally good books, one by an older and trustworthy person and one by a young and beautiful one, they will often choose the latter because they have two cards to play with when promoting the book – strong book and sexy young looks. (Old folks can look sexy too, but it's the facial skin that counts.) The other reason is that agents know that publishers invest a lot in a writer when they choose to publish him or her, and are reluctant to publish a book when the likelihood of it being followed by a second one are slim. A little cruel, but possibly true.

Of course, none of us know the hour of our death, but still, on the whole, statistics count. As Fran McCullough puts it, "The problem with novelists is that they're either successful with their first book, or they have to wait until the fourth or fifth. If you're a seventy-year-old novelist, waiting until the fourth or fifth book is problematic."

Recently I had a conversation with a publisher about a manuscript I had submitted. He told me that he was interested but that the publishing house's schedule was full for the next two years. There was a pause and then he asked me, "Will you still be alive two years from now?" I quickly replied that I thought I would be having a new book of poetry coming out then and certainly planned to be around. Only now do I reflect on the audacity of his question when he, himself, has no idea when death will call on him. But if you're determined to be published, perhaps you had better be alert and keep those grey hairs out of your curriculum vitae. I should also point out that as far as ageism goes, grants, fellowships and attendance at writer's colonies often have age limitations, so if you are a first-time writer at the age of 63, you might have trouble when applying for any of these.

As I said at the beginning of this chapter, as far as creativity goes, ageism doesn't count so strongly. The advice to a writer is always to write about what you know, so apart from your special areas of interest, certainly if you are writing about aging, or older people, then you are an authority and that counts in your favour. Ah! If only we were indexers, instead of writers: indexers are still needed, in spite of the Internet, and their average age is late 50s!

I like Robert Bly's idea, "I believe that every time a young writer gets an award, he should look around for an older writer, probably poorer than he is, and give a tenth of it to him, or her." Bly also suggests the reverse and that brings in the pleasant idea of writers supporting and encouraging each other.

2 *Let's begin*

A room of one's own

When I first thought of writing full-time, my ideas did not immediately spring to one small room where I could write my heart out. They dwelt on a wider environment that might have the degree of isolation and quietness I needed (or rather thought I needed) for the perfect conditions to write. Moving to an island, as I eventually did, definitely cut out a number of distracting factors such as pollution and noise. The move to Gabriola also gave me pluses such as a natural environment to work in and a supportive small community in which I could find a modest niche.

So within my new island home, I prepared my own writing space. Each morning I cleaned my desk, opened a fresh file on the computer, laid a writing pad and sharpened pencils beside it, found a comfy office chair...and then I would go downstairs, lie on the couch, cover myself with the afghan I had knitted for my husband, and start to write.

But generally, if you can (and wish to) have your own writing space, try and reserve that space solely for writing.

Try to do no other activity there. The area should have the smell you want – fresh flowers, dogs at your feet or cat in your lap, hot coffee (or herb tea) at your elbow; and the view you want – no windows at all, or looking out on to greenery, the beach, humanity – whatever helps. The smells and textures with which you surround yourself may be familiar ones from the past that will help the memories to come flooding back (if memoirs are what you are writing). The clean desk, the stack of reference books, familiar pictures on the wall may provide the sense of security that you require in order to begin writing. Alternatively, piles of papers and manuscripts strewn over all the available surfaces, as well as the floor, may provide the degree of chaos that you prefer to float in.

Another option, this time outside the home, is to reserve that small table in your local coffee shop where humanity passing by is your stimulus. Or again, somewhere close to the setting you have chosen for your novel – an airport, a shopping mall, a seniors' centre – might be the perfect place for you to choose.

Whichever space you select, be sure to pile up beside you a good dictionary, thesaurus and style book. For dictionary, I use Random House, second edition, and have it placed open on an unusual lectern – a hospital tray that usually slides over a hospital bed, but, in our crowded double-office, slides over a filing cabinet, keeping everything compact, but easily available. As far as thesauruses, *Roget's Thesaurus* is the standard, and for a book on style I prefer that slender classic, *The Elements of Style,* by William Strunk Jr. and E. B. White, a one time editor of *The New Yorker* magazine.

E. B. White, who wrote with great clarity himself, once stated that if those who have studied the art of writing are in accord on one point it is on this: the surest way to arouse and hold the reader is to be specific, definite and concrete. Great advice from a great stylist.

You can augment this basic collection of reference books with any number of books on style, as for example *Writing with Style* by Shirley I. Pautian. Grammar and punctuation are things most people don't talk about much after they have finished school, unless it is in books like the best-seller *Eats, Shoots and Leaves* by Lynne Truss – a fun book on punctuation. There are many books out there, however, that are helpful for refreshing your English-class memories, such as Margaret Shertzer's *The Elements of Grammar.*

Even with over 30 books under my belt, I still find great pleasure in reading books that give advice on how to write. I usually do this at times when I have writer's block, only to find that I have become entrapped in other writers' lives and am sunk even more deeply into my own inertia at the end of it all, rather than being inspired to jump into my computer chair and get going. So be warned, don't use the need to study style as another procrastination excuse.

The above advice on a suitable writing space is for all writers, not just those of you starting a little late in life. In fact, for you Late Bloomers' the space has probably been chosen long ago. It was just waiting for you to declare yourself.

Capturing ideas and encouraging the muse

Now you have your space picked and your reference books handy, let's have a look at things that will further your actual writing process. Where do ideas come from? They come from everywhere and at anytime and so will yours, but will you remember that great idea you had at two o'clock in the morning? "At night you can be surprised by words," states Sophy Burnham, and how right she is! As we age, parts of our memories stand out so clearly that we can touch and taste and smell them. Other recollections fuse together, or come up hazy. Better safe than sorry is the appropriate cliché here, so when the idea comes, write it down immediately.

Based on that advice, I keep pads of paper, pens and sharpened pencils for recording and Hasti-Notes for marking pages everywhere: in the kitchen, my place at the dining table, in the living room, the office, the bedroom (beside a lounge chair, and at my bedside) and in the bathroom. As you are writing your ideas down, make sure you give enough details so that when you look at the note later on, you are not completely bemused. Often I will read in my notebooks such phrases as: "Jumping the gap" or "Don't need marking," and haven't the slightest idea what they could possibly mean.

Every so often, I gather up all the notes and my thoughts for poems or essays from around the house and take them up to my desk and enter them on the machine in suitable places. I have a file for lines that would be great in poems yet to be written; a file for quotes from current reading material that are more apt, witty or wise than anything I could ever produce; a file for gossip and island stories that I jot down as soon as tea-drinking friends and neighbours depart; a file for philosophical musings that usually come up when I'm knitting... Well you get the idea. It's amazing what a collection of useful material turns up this way. Hold yourself open, and keep those pencils sharp.

After the practicalities of room and recording are settled, then the writer has to consider their own *modus operandi* – writing everyday at the same time, or writing when the muse strikes and doing other things until she does.

There is an old joke: a stranger to New York asked the violinist, Jascha Heifitz "How do you get to Carnegie Hall?" Heifitz answered, "Practice!" And while this applies to a certain degree to a writer as well as a violinist, every book presents a new problem and writing is not exactly like learning to ride a bike (or play a violin)!

The Latin adage runs *nulla dies sine linea* (never a day without a line), originally this meant an artist's line, but it applies well to the writing life. Guy de Maupassant exhorted, "Get black on white," while Natalie Goldberg urges, "keep your hand moving." You may be doing this already, having entered daily notes in your journal for years and you will probably continue doing so. If not, why not consider the possibility?

There are, however, other approaches that might suit you better. For example, Kipling took the second approach: "drift, wait and obey the daemon within." I go for this approach myself and fill the rest of my time with writing query letters to editors, booking my readings in public, planning my workshops...and knitting.

To add to this I take Emily Dickinson's recommendation to heart and add time for daydreaming and reverie, although she recommends this for making a prairie and I for the making of a writer.

So we have exponents of daily writing practice and exponents of dreaming. Agatha Christie suggested doing other kinds of activities as the best way to get started: "The best time for planning a book is while you're doing the dishes," she said.

Somehow doing the chores brings up in us a great desire to be doing something else. If the urge is strong enough, by the time the dishes are done, or the laundry is folded and put away, or a garden bed turned, we will have the plan for a new story, a new poem, a new book buzzing away in our minds.

Usually I do a bit of this and a bit of that. My rhythms change too much for regular daily writing, so while I often write for an hour or two every morning, sometimes I choose to garden instead, or do some fabric work. I like to make a distinction between writing and real writing. The first is fine, but the second is rarer. It occurs when the writing comes out almost in spite of you, and no matter how much you resist, the writing demands to be written. It becomes the most important thing in your life, even though parts of you may be embarrassed, or even ashamed, at what is going down on the page. The well has blown and the oil just continues to pour out.

It is that overwhelming feeling of almost explosion, that 'wait until you just can't wait any longer because the words are piling up in your mouth threatening to burst out' feeling I need before I can usefully sit down to write. But although I don't belong to the practice every day school, I do jot down a poem, or an idea for a poem or an essay almost every day, though the hours when I do so may vary wildly.

While we are considering ways of encouraging the muse, I should mention that there are many books available with exercises to loosen your right brain and to shake you up, such as Patricia Cummings suggestion, "Write a postcard in a language you don't understand. Translate it." I have listed a few interesting books of this sort in the bibliography at the end.

Calvin Coolidge seems to be returning to the idea of the daily quota of words in the following excerpt, but really he is talking about persistence, a quality in urgent need once you have begun writing: "Nothing in the world can take the place of Persistence. Talent will not; nothing is more common than unsuccessful men with talent. Genius will not; unrewarded genius is almost a proverb. Education will not; the world is full of educated derelicts. Persistence and determination alone are omnipotent."

Recently, a local writer was telling me how he was discovered. He was reading from his work in a coffee house when a writer approached him and asked whether he had any more writing like the selection he had chosen to read. He said he had two novels lined up and a third on its way. On the strength of that, and being very struck with his reading, the writer approached her publisher. The publisher was similarly impressed, not just by the quality of the work, but also by the fact that the author had already written two whole books entirely on speculation, no contract in view, just with the persistence that he needed in order to write them. It pays to show you've put out some effort before you approach a publisher.

Once you've thought of something you'd like to write, unless you have already found your own voice (more on this in a moment), I suggest you start by imitating other writers. Imitate – everyone does (but be careful not to plagiarize). You will, of course, start by imitating the style of your favourite authors, poets or playwrights.

Three poets I really like are Wislawa Szymborska (Poland), Billy Collins (USA) and John West (Australia). Their poetry resonates with me and reinforces my desire to write of small everyday matters, ask difficult questions and be as compassionate as I can without being maudlin. I had read most everything they have written and then, one day, I stopped reading them and started writing. My own poetry now bears only slight resemblance to any of these three poets, but I still nod my head in their direction from time to time, acknowledging their influence and thanking them for their distinctive voices. In writing, gratitude is important.

But what if you don't have a favourite author, or you are afraid that if you do get one, their style will overpower your own? Yes, that seems to be a problem for some, but for me the act of admiring other authors doesn't threaten a swamping of my own talent. Rather it empowers it with the thought that, in my own small way, I too am part of that wonderful body of poets or essayists that can make some change for the better by the wise use of words. Parents often are reluctant to have a second child because they feel they will not have enough love available to be able to love it as much as they do the first, but when they do actually have one, they find there is more than enough love to go round. It's like that with writing. Even though you respect your own work, you will respect it even more by seeing how it fits into the wider world of writers both past and present. Please believe me on this point.

On voice

Now to the gist of writing. That is not just to find the most agreeable way of working, but to find your own voice. Don't worry about being a good writer, or about being exciting, original and witty. Worry about being you. "Be yourself. The world worships the original," Ingrid Bergman expounded. The first part of her statement I agree with, but trying to be original is not really what writing's about. Striving for originality produces contrived and very faddish writing, I feel, while writing with your own voice produces writing with true integrity. Allow your humanity full play – be ambivalent, look at awkward questions, talk about things people don't usually talk about, but that are important to you.

Sometimes when a writer whose voice had been inhibited finds it, at first it may appear rather strident and opinionated. As an antidote for any dogmatism that may creep into my writing, I like to write a point of view and then support the opposite point of view. Niels Bohr, who was concerned with being fair and balanced, often used the last part of a sentence to modify the first part. That's what I mean.

The advantage of starting later in life is that the knocks and blows and pats and praises you have received have already encouraged that still small voice to emerge, though perhaps slowly and timidly. Nevertheless, it has probably shown moments of manifestation, or at least that is what I hope. While writing with your authentic voice is not quite the same as writing to please yourself, I can say with some certainty that if you write to please others, you will never find your own voice. Why bother saying things that you think people will expect you to say, or want you to say? Why settle for lies or half-truths? Emily Dickinson advised, "Tell all the truth but tell it slant," but more of that later when we come to discuss how much to tell.

The integrity I seek in my writing came when I had recovered my own voice. I write 'recovered' for, of course, it was there all the while, only just not permitted out.

3 What shall you write?

You don't need a Wow! experience

Having found your voice, two things become of concern. The first is that you make sure your voice does not disappear through heavy editing by others. A friend of mine dictated her memoirs to a secretary, who then rewrote and modified them. When the memoirs went to the publisher, they were again edited and my friend's lively voice was nowhere to be found in the finished book. Guard your voice carefully. The second thing to think about, when your voice is coming through clearly, is the more exciting consideration of what to write about.

When I had reached this stage, I did an analysis for myself that clarified my writing aims and subjects. I am including it here in the hopes that it may also offer you ideas for discovering where you would like to go with your writing, and what subjects you might enjoy writing about.

As encouragement I reminded myself of the William Zinsser quotation, "Readers and editors and agents don't know what they want to read until they read it. If it's important to you, it will be important to other people." So what was important to me? This is what I wrote at that time:

> From time to time I check out what the rest of the world is reading and writing about. Recently I came up with a list. It contained writings on brothels in Tehran, on the concentration camps, on the internment camps, on AIDS, on incest (well, always on incest!)...the list went on and on and, whilst intriguing material, it left me puzzling. Although all of a certain interest, I had very little I could actually write about on any of these topics.
>
> I had always heard, you should write about what you know. "And what might that be?" I wondered. All I know is maybe. I started to make a list of what I might know enough about...enough, that is, to perhaps patch together a reasonable essay.
>
> • Restlessness and moments of extreme discontent that strangely increase in intensity with age, as, overall and paradoxically, the still centre of my being gets stronger and my general contentment increases.
>
> • Haiku writing (and reading). Yes, I know a good haiku when I see one. The sigh that comes up from who knows where and, when it does, the whole world falls into place. Once in a while I can even

produce a good haiku. Once in a while, when I am totally wrapped up with weeding or scrubbing the kitchen floor or planning a quilt, a haiku will appear and knock me over with its simplicity and revelation.

- Cleaning up messes, yes! The fact that I have caused the mess in the first place is irrelevant. The greater the mess the more I enjoy writing about how I throw things around, and out, and make piles, and file papers until a work space, or leisure place appears and invites. It was there all the while of course, just layered with junk like our Buddha nature is, or so I am told.

- Then when all is straight, I can write about moving things from here to there in the interest of beauty. How I placed a few golden leaves on the breakfast cloth, the pleasure of putting fresh towels in the bathroom, or lavender in a basket at the door – no, not that side, this is where people's eyes will alight as they come up to the door. I can write about small nudges into beauty like that.

- Being a twin. Yes, I can certainly write about being a twin. I can imagine the division of the egg, the battle for our mother's meagre food, the birth cry of she who came out first and the terror of the one left behind in the womb. The babies in the double pram who knew that when a spasmodic kick touched flesh, another being was somewhere near, and the joy of a fantasy childhood where my sister's and my own small created world saved us from the larger one outside the garden fence. Desertion when separate partners were found and the attempts to make the partner over into the twin one had really lost by choice. Yes, I can write about twins.

- Life on a small island. Why not? After all that is where I have been living for the past ten years. Although to write freely I will have to wait until I leave the island, because I am careless and forget to change names and slightly alter situations, at least beyond recognition.

- Small children. There are few in our neck of the woods, but still I feel the imprint of my daughter's hand around my neck every time I put on a warm scarf and every time I look up into our excellent country darkness, I see my son's earnest little face when he demanded to know why there were holes in the sky. So, yes! I have a few things to write about children.

Well, restlessness, haiku, making messes, cleaning up messes, beautiful touches, twins, my small island, my children when young – not such a bad beginning. It's not the brothels of Tehran, but it's plenty enough material to stop my whining about writer's block and start those computer keys bouncing. Small things, if written about from the heart, contain bigger things is my philosophy. So not having had Wow! experiences to tap in your life doesn't mean you can't be a writer, and a fine one at that.

As I always like to look at a situation from several angles, having firmly decided on what I could write about, Paul Klee's quotation sprang into my mind: "When I paint what you know, I bore you. When I paint what I know, I bore me. So I paint what I don't know." Now, how about that! Where's your list of topics?

Once you have chosen a topic, or list of topics to write about, what form should your writing take? Poetry, essays, fiction?

I won't dwell on how to get started because 50, 60, 70 years worth of writing is stored up inside you ready to come out. That's why you picked up this book to read. But what form should your writing take? Only reading can tell. I mean that when you read a novel, a mystery, a poetry book, a book of essays and you resonate so that you want to hold that book in your hands forever, then that is probably the form you should choose for your own writing.

Finding your form

It might help you to hear how I chose haiku for my first solid poetry writing attempts in my late 50s. My journey into form reads as a kind of breathless period, and it was.

For several years I let myself flow from one experience to another around the globe, until I eventually found myself solidly-grounded in both living place and writing choice, on our small property on Gabriola, from where I have barely moved for the last 10 years.

I got lost in haiku when I lived in Japan and here I trace back, and forward, how I came to choose haiku as my main writing form, just as later, you will see clearly why you chose the form you did for your writing.

I came to haiku via Buddhism and Japan. I came to Buddhism by rushing to the Himalayas, looking for I know not what, and finding Vajrayana Buddhism in grubby Buddhist monasteries. I drank out of skulls and meditated on thigh bones, all to no avail. Later to Japan…still in search. Zen monasteries full of hollow-chested, schizoid *gaijin* (foreigners) and no sign of *wabi-sabi* in the stuffed subways of that country.

Back in Canada, trying to sort out what had been gained, I wrote several books about things Japanese and one book wrote me, *Haiku – one breath poetry.* In this book, my Buddhist training in Vipassana and the whiffs of aesthetics I received in Japan combined to at last grant me a few insights. It didn't surprise me that the book became a favourite with librarians and teachers and was listed on many haiku web sites.

Sales of *Haiku – one breath poetry,* and our other books allowed my husband and me to move to the island of Gabriola. Here, at last, I came to realize that householder's chores were the perfect basis for insight meditation practice. Moreover, the simple life I adopted, necessitated by a large mortgage late in life, allowed me to understand, at last, *wabi-sabi* (a kind of beauty that illustrates impermanence) and other such Japanese subtleties.

> **why go**
> **to Tokyo, when the dream**
> **happened here?**
> *Naomi Beth Wakan*

Watching the seasons more closely, by necessity again, I learned about the coming into being and the passing away of all things. In moments of weeding concentration and mending concentration and cleaning concentration, a few haiku jumped through the gaps. Enough to produce hubris, but only the rare hair-standing-on-end haiku. Still, the flow of *mini-satori* moments had begun. I lost all desire for the Himalayas, and even for the ferry trip to take me to the nearest island, Vancouver Island.

I met up with other *haijin* (haiku writers) and read their miraculous moments too. With the small worlds of haiku-writing, essay-writing, longer-poetry writing and playing with fabric, I have almost recovered the promising young child who created her own world so long ago, because the one around her was so inconsistent.

> **from washbasin**
> **to washbasin, all**
> **is nonsense**
>
> *Issa*

> **In Heaven**
> **and on earth**
> **Laughter and tears,**
> **Laughter and tears**
>
> *Torei*

> **the little monk**
> **jumps into the void**
> **smiling**
>
> *Naomi Beth Wakan*

> **after the garden party...the garden**
> *Ruth Yarrow*

You may have long ago chosen the form you want to write and so probably won't have to take the circuitous journey I had to take. Nevertheless, you might want to reflect for a moment on what has lead you to contemplate the writing life in general, a particular form of the writing life, or at least taking pen to paper, or opening the computer to write down some memories you'd like to record. The backward journey may jog you forward along the next trail.

Exploring my forms: poetry and essays

As, late in life, I chose the haiku form, along with blank verse and essays, as the way I could best express myself, I'd like to explore the haiku form a little further to perhaps help you to feel out which form might best suit your here and now, by giving myself as example.

My husband was reading an old Buckminster Fuller book, *Critical Path*. He loves large ponderous tomes that he savours slowly after each meal. In the foreword he came across that beautiful piece by e.e.cummings, *A Poet's Advice*, which finishes, "and so my advice to all young people who wish to be poets is: do something easy, like learning how to blow up the world – unless you're not only willing, but glad, to feel and work and fight until you die."

cummings speaks of "expressing nobody-but-yourself," and there's the rub. I have spent most of my years trying to find the authentic me and no matter how many onion-layers I peel off, there still seems to be plenty of pretence and posturing around. That's why I like writing haiku, why I favour this deceptively simple form of poetry.

As you may have noticed I am somewhat loose with words, in fact they flow endlessly from my mouth. I use them to keep people from looking inside and also to seduce and charm them into getting nearer. I use them to make readers laugh and to make them sigh and shed a few tears at the sadness of it all. I use them, I hope, so that the reader will seize a pen to write down one of my haiku that may change their life forever, or at least divert them for the moment.

And moment is what haiku is mostly about. Haiku are not full of reflections on the past, or fantasies of the future. They are entirely concerned with where you are at a particular moment in time: the smell, taste, feel, sound and sight of the moment, its greenness and woolliness and chirpiness and perfume and sweetness. For me, who has spent most of my life in some parallel universe of dreams, the haiku form is a great discipline and a wonderful grounding device.

Limiting myself to a few words in order to describe an infinite moment proved to be very easy once I set my mind to it. The price was right for my simple life – one needed only a bit of paper and a pencil, and sometimes even that wasn't necessary.

> **No paper!**
> **I write a haiku**
> **on a shell.**
>
> *Naomi Beth Wakan*

Living in Japan provided the impetus for my haiku writing. I read the great three, Bashō, Buson and Issa feverishly; and even went to Iga Ueno and looked longingly into Bashō's little room in the house where he was born. I was, however, a little disillusioned to find that after the initial speedy recording of the haiku, great haiku poets often took many years to perfect their seventeen simple syllables. Another letdown was to find that my Japanese students often slipped into their pockets earlier-prepared haiku and took them along to competitions, where the essence was supposed to be spontaneity!

At death, the poet (and the samurai) were expected – in the good old days – to provide a half-decent haiku; and these too, I'm afraid to tell you, were often written in good health many years before.

I am basically a lazy person. I rush around doing a lot so that people will think I am occupied and not just an idle bum. The idea of expressing a deeply profound image within the limits of three lines strikes me as a wonderful economy of energy. Haiku make the everyday sacred and since I am an everyday, ordinary kind of person, it amuses me to think that I have such a powerful tool at hand. A tool I share with some of the greatest poets in the world and one that compares favourably with the verbosity and pomposity of many so-called philosophers.

Although a haiku can seize you anywhere, living in the country and near the seashore allows me to stay somewhat within the traditional school in which each haiku must refer to a natural phenomenon. A haiku is about one incident, at one moment in time, and that time is the present. All the rest is petty rules from poetry-teaching tyrants. As John Gardner so aptly put it, "Most supposed aesthetic rules prove relative under pressure." I could continue in this vein forever and that is why I prefer to write haiku, than to write about them.

**One writes
because everyone cannot see
goldfish playing**

Naomi Beth Wakan

If you haven't settled into it yet, I wonder what form your writing will take?

If you are choosing to write poetry, haiku is only one of many poetic forms you might select. I prefer blank verse for my longer poems. If writing haiku is not for you, how about trying a cinquain, ballad, blank verse, canto, elegy, epigram, epistle, epitaph, ghazal, lyric, ode, parody, prose poem, sestina, sonnet, villanelle...why the names alone could make a wonderful poem. No, I'm not going to describe them, for http://thewordshop.tripod.com/forms.html tells it all. Books such as John Whitworth's *Writing Poetry* are also useful.

"Poetry is an island that breaks away from the main."
– Derek Walcott

When I'm not writing poetry, essays are my favourite form. The essay is a great form for the beginning older writer to launch into because there are a wealth of topics to choose from among your careers, interests, hobbies, holidays and family ups and downs. Essays can take the form of travelogues, of giving advice on a particular topic, or may just consist of your own creative musings.

Topics lie around you in every room of the house. Why are toilet paper and paper towel embossed? What do bar codes tell us? Why do we have Social Security numbers? (That could get into murkier waters.) Further afield, the garden and community suggest a host of topics that would make great small essays for which a range of magazines must be urgently awaiting. I'll speak of magazines later when I talk about submitting work, but a little research will find just the magazine for almost any topic. I once found a very fine magazine that only took literary articles about gardens – not 'how to prune the roses,' but 'what Aunt Rose found at the bottom of the garden' sort of articles. I happened to have just such an article and got a cheque in the return mail – almost unheard of in the world of magazines.

In school I was deeply influenced by the essays of Lamb and of Addison and Steele, the *De Coverly Papers* and the *Spectator* magazine. I thought, how wonderful to choose a theme, develop it, throw in a few relevant quotations, an ending that echoed the beginning and have an essay. Little did I know that years later James Burke, in his Connections column in Scientific American, would develop my circular essay to its excruciating extreme repetitiveness.

Once the essay topic is chosen, the research begins. Some writers like to jot down random thoughts on the subject first and then check out the accuracy of their facts and add a few relevant quotes. Others start by searching the subject they have chosen with Google, looking for an interesting angle or a startling way to begin. The first and last sentences in an essay, as in a 1000 page novel, are the ones that stick in the mind.

On novels

And speaking of novels, perhaps some of you have a story lingering in your heart and are yearning to write a fine novel. I, myself, have only written one fiction book and that was for young children. As far as reading fiction goes, detective stories are my choice for relaxation when I'm not reading poetry and physics. So while I can't give you personal advice on writing fiction, I can point you in the direction of a writer who teaches and writes about fiction writing, who is clear, concise and covers a wide area of writing matters. Her name is Donna Levin, and in *Get that Novel Started* and *Get that Novel Written* she will probably answer most of your pressing questions on fiction writing. I have provided other useful titles in this area in the bibliography.

I'm told the ideal novel has twelve chapters of thirty pages each. I prefer to read smaller chapters myself, as I (in Puritan fashion) alternate the reward of a chapter of reading with housework. If the chapters are too long, the house tends to fall into disarray while my absorption is elsewhere.

The general advice to novelists is to get it all down first. Donna Levin describes this amusingly: "Writing the first draft of a novel is like going over Niagara Falls in a barrel. As you huddle in that barrel you are not overly concerned with the form of your plunge – you just want to make it to the bottom – and out of the barrel – alive." She adds that, "when you've finished the first draft, you're a novelist... Tinkering around for two years with an opening chapter does not a novelist make..."

As to plot, I quote E. M. Forster, "Yes – oh, dear, yes, a novel tells a story." Donna Levin defines plot for you as "a series of causally related events that emerge from a series of ever-intensifying conflicts and prove a premise at the end." Plots must involve conflict and here Donna advises that, "the best stories will contain conflict in which both parties are right, or at least have a good case to state."

As to character writing, I like Oakley Hall's advice a lot: "It is not sufficient to assemble a character by adding characteristics as grilles and fenders might be added on an assembly line... The character must be produced on the page, whole and alive, his breath congealing on the air." The main character, of course, should be page centre and in the middle of the action, even if he/she hasn't taken the action him/herself.

Some writers think that style can make up for a weak plot and characters. It can't. No matter how witty you are, how cleverly you move back and forward in time, alternate short and long chapters, brilliant chapter titles – whatever your scintillating choice – bad writing is bad writing. Oakley Hall's wise comment should be noted, "Perhaps the writer's true style begins to emerge when he [she] makes no deliberate effort to produce one."

For a commercially successful book, happy endings are often required with the bad guys eliminated, or at least punished, and the good guys rewarded with – everlasting love, the family inheritance, you name it. But we, with the wisdom of seniors, are not concerned with worldly success, are we? So the ending is open for us, since we are almost certain that Cinderella and her Prince found their relationship strained from time to time, and we know for sure that the meek rarely inherit the earth.

Joan Bolker tells you firmly that, "the unread story is not a story; it is little black marks on wood pulp. The reader, reading it, makes it live: a live thing, a story." So if you've got a good tale in your head, or in your desk drawer, make it a story soon; the reader is waiting.

If true romance is where you think your talent lies, I strongly recommend Vanessa Grant's book, *Writing Romance.* It is full of helpful lists – successful ingredients for a romance novel, requirement lists for plot germination and lists of categories of romance writing. Vanessa, who lived on my island of Gabriola, used it as background for some of the more than 25 Harlequin romances she has written. Islands are hot beds for romance plots although, I must say, our island seems somewhat lacking in available heroes.

Last bit of advice, this time by Robert Frost: "No surprise for the writer, no surprise for the reader."

4 Memoirs

> *"The biographer's problem is that he never knows enough, the autobiographer that he knows too much."*
> — Russell Baker

Memoir writing is often chosen as a starting form for older writers. Usually it is in order to leave a recorded heritage for offspring. Sometimes it is just that – a straight record, sometimes it's a justification, sometimes a reformation, sometimes an attempt at reconciliation, sometimes just a way of sorting out your life.

For whatever reasons they are written, memoirs are a very accessible form of writing, since they are yours and are stored within your head, your heart and your guts. William Zinsser, however, points out helpfully that, "an interesting life doesn't make an interesting memoir. Only small pieces of life make an interesting memoir." So if the task seems overwhelming, start with a small piece; it may have shaped your whole life.

Describing one incident in place and time can, indeed, be used to tell a whole lot more than just that incident. It can indicate how your life changed at that point, how an interest started or faded away, how a relationship bittered or sweetened. Autobiography is usually done sequentially starting with birth, or even conception. Of course it doesn't have to be that way. You can start at any point and jog back and forward as the sequence takes you. There is no right place to begin. Just start and it will all gradually fall into place.

It is important, however, at whichever point in time you begin, to let your reader know clearly when places and times that you are describing change. You are inviting them on a journey, and you want to be a clear guide. Paul Levitt said that, "Writing is the process of naming a particular world into existence." In this case, the particular world is your past.

In *Memory Bag,* a book I wrote to help people write their memoirs, I go over the various decisions to be made before beginning, such as how much to tell, whom to include and how to get going. Then I include a series of questions to jog your memory along its path – on childhood, leaving home, partners, etc. I also tell how to shape the memoirs up and get them ready for publication.

Here I would like, for a moment, to discuss the writing process. Some people feel recording an interview facilitates the flow of memories as the tongue loosens in the telling of old tales to an audience. So consider the use of a tape recorder when you start out on your memoirs, but if someone else is writing it down, please remember my warning about losing your voice in the process.

With memoirs or autobiography, photographs, home videos, letters, postcards, souvenirs, old newspapers, year books and diaries are endless sources for material. So, unless you've led a very wandering life, as I have, you should have lots of raw material on hand, in the attic or the guest room cupboards. For research outside the home, revisiting places of the past – birthplace, schools, honeymoon hotel, etc. – will trigger endless memories. For facts, there are government records, local archives and genealogical tables.

While you may prefer to jot down memories on a writing-pad, the computer is the best place to store them. Each person or time period can be given its own file, which will soon fill up with additions. That way all those loose pieces of paper will be replaced by neat computer files under the general directory MEMOIRS. They can then be easily shifted around into the order you feel is best when you are putting it all together.

Getting all the facts down is a beginning, but it isn't enough. The memoir will be boring if you don't comment on incidents and places, how they affected your thinking, or changed your way of behaving. The raw material is the framework. Your readers will want to share your strivings and decisions.

Recently I started collecting the poetry of other poets that, from my childhood, has mattered to me. As the poems slipped into my file, the memories started flooding back. From A.A. Milne's *Vespers* to Yeat's *The Lake Isle of*

Innisfree to William Carlos Williams' *The Red Wheelbarrow* to Billy Collins' *Introduction to Poetry* and John West's *Hospital Two-step,* I could have written an autobiography based on poetry alone.

"Memory, one of the most powerful of writer's tools is one of the most unreliable," William Zinsser reminds us. Within the family each member recalls an incident differently; even twins know this only too well. So don't fret that you may not be getting it all down correctly, fret that you may not be getting it down at all.

Kiss and tell

When people start to consider the possibility of getting their memoirs down, whether it is as poetry, fiction or, most likely, as a straight recording, the question, "How frank do I want to be?" usually crosses their mind. How firmly your little censor is sitting on your shoulder is really the consideration here. Bernard Malamud said that all biography is ultimately fiction and I suppose the same could be said about autobiography and memoir writing. Omission is after all a form of untruth now, isn't it? So let's take a concentrated look at memoir writing in respect to the truth, the whole truth, and nothing but the truth.

A friend recently wrote his memories of a section of his life. On reading it over he realised that although he had written in detail about the birth of four of his children, he hadn't mentioned the fifth. Should he have? Would you in similar circumstances? Does one have to give each member of the family the same number of pages when writing memoirs? Well yes, if the little critic is sitting on your shoulder. That is the critic that has stopped you from doing a number of things that might have been interesting, if not fun, in your lifetime and there it is still sitting there telling you what to write!

William Zinsser warns, "This fear of family disapproval keeps many family histories from being written." Although he also complains of the 1990s when "no episode was too sordid, no family too dysfunctional, to be trotted out for the wonderment of the masses..."

Even if you are writing fiction, are people going to assume your fictional characters are all taken from you and your family? Do you really care? Or perhaps you only thinly spread on the fiction so that people would recognize what a wild and wonderful/terrible, or distressing/dull and ordinary family you had. However thick the veneer, it is recommended in fiction that no names bear a resemblance to anyone in your family or your community.

Besides changing names, if you must use family or community figures in your writing (and why not, that is the material at hand), shuffle them around like those old-fashioned children's books where the pages were cut in three so you could interchange heads, middles and legs. That is, take traits from various friends and family and assign them to a miscellany of characters so any one figure in your story might have the habits of an uncle, a stepfather and the local supermarket produce-manager combined.

Whether you have fictionalised your memoirs, or written them in non-fiction format, are you getting too close to the closet for your children's, your ex-spouse's or your second cousin's liking? That is a decision you alone (or their lawyers) can make. A writing instructor once told me that I had to choose between my friends and family and my craft. Sitting on the fence as ever, I chose somewhere in between.

David Rakoff speaks of memoirs "brushed with sepia"; and that's how most of mine are, I'm afraid. But, if you are telling secrets you've promised never to divulge, I suggest heavy disguise both for you and your writing and don't ever promise to keep anything secret again.

But besides truth in memoirs, the critic on the shoulder can come up in other ways in any form of writing. How many four-letter words do you want to use, even if that is the natural language of your characters? How clearly do you want to describe anatomy in scenes of sexual splendour? How perverted can your characters be while you stay coolly on the sidelines watching them? That critic asks endless questions. The elder writer often has cast aside the significance of these questions...don't forget you can wear purple and spit in the gutter. I want to add to this that if you can push your critic-on-the-shoulder off your shoulder and stop evaluating your work as you go along, you will be surprised at how your creativity flows and how smoothly the truth can be presented.

Have I written my memoirs? Well, no, not exactly. A little shamefacedly after selling the umpteenth copy of *Memory Bag*, I set about writing a brief poem covering 74 years. It turned out to have just a few more lines than my years. Now when people ask that question, I can smile and say, "Yes, actually, I have." I wrote my poem-memoir in the third person to perhaps defuse the intensity for me a little and, yes, I actually forgot to mention my twin sister and guiltily slipped her in at the end.

A brief autobiography

**Refusing to enter
this vale of horrors,
she was dragged out
whimpering between
a pair of forceps and
thrust into an incubator.
Her uncertain birth was
not registered for several
months and for the rest
of her life she felt
that she might die
at any moment. This caused
her to reluctantly commit
herself to anything more
than short term ventures.
She skimmed through school
and college and fearing
her imminent death and
greedy to survive, and**

be survived, she married
and produced two children.
Moulded by her mother and
stepsisters to be a melding of
Mahatma Gandhi, Mother Theresa
and the Russian mother of the year,
she woke up at forty and remembered
that she had really wanted
to be Ginger Rogers. She then
turned the supper upside down
on the table and walked out.
She bought herself red shoes
a frilly dress and castanets,
and flamencoed through
the next two years, alternating
dance with horse back riding
and a string of young men.
Then, having won her teen years
back, years lost to Bernard Shaw,
the Spanish Civil War and the
slum dwellers of Birmingham,
she remarried and immediately
learned about shovels and saws
and poverty, and how to listen
to country music and other skills.
All this linked her closer
to the vale of tears she had
not wanted to enter those
many years before. In her 60s
she remembered how to play
and spent days making little books
and painting second-rate folk art.

One day she found her mammary glands
had let her down and, standing on
her head, she changed her diet
and her doctor and plunged
into the life of her small community.

She wrote endless poems about death
that frightened her writers' group
and, deciding to leave her boobs
in position, she annoyed all
the islanders who hadn't.
She started to sell her second-rate art,
which began to have
the appearance of first-rate
and got four books published
in one year, a feat to match
the greatest (although the print runs were small).
She made two quilts and read 15
John Le Carré spy stories, then
deciding to extol her simple
lifestyle, she settled down
to write essays on clotheslines and tofu.
A few years later,
admitting a certain defeat,
she had her right breast removed
and wrote some brilliant haiku
on the whole procedure and
some touching poems
afterwards.
Her poems grew richer and deeper
and her still, small voice
ricocheted across Canada,
if not the world.
She decided the garden was not
an examination site, nor
her daily meals open
to food critics, thus lightening
her load, she continued
writing about tofu and seaweed
and added pin tucks to
the subject matter.
Did she mention that
she had a twin?
(to be continued)

5 *Frameworks and editing*

Something to hang your writing on

Robert Wallace asks, "Why do we value form? Perhaps the answer lies in the secrets of our musculature, in our dark roots. Why do we live in square rooms? Why do we draw mechanical doodles when we are bored? Why do we tap our feet to music? Perhaps there is a profound link between the meter of verse and the human pulse, the rhythm of life itself."

With this in mind, we should carefully choose a form of writing that resonates with us; that will best complement our words. The form is the larger unit – poetry (and subforms of poetry), essays, fiction, non-fiction, educational writing, journalism, or writing for young adults. Having chosen the form, we should next give ourselves a framework within the form, which supplies a more intricate structure on which to hang our words. For example, after having chosen poetry as a form in which to express myself, I selected haiku as a subform. When I come to write a haiku, I know that I have to tell what is happening, where it is happening and when. This is the framework I use within the three lines that haiku usually takes when written in English. By now, I do not consciously need to draw this framework up as an outline, as I would in the case of when I write an essay, for it is embedded in my mind.

Recently I chose the essay form for a light, amusing piece about my attempts to write a cookbook. The framework for this piece was the list of dietary changes I had made over the years I had been attempting to write (and finish) a cookbook. Each dietary change necessitated a complete change of recipes, so the framework for my essay form became – vegetarian, vegan, macrobiotics, finishing up with my present diet, non-dairy + chicken + fish. Having the framework in place before I began made the writing process very smooth.

For we writers starting later in life, all the props we can find are helpful. So unless you are taking the plunge into free-form, stream of consciousness writing, take time to draw up your framework before you begin. It will save you having to sort out a mess of unstructured writing later on.

Using a framework doesn't just help the older writer. It also helps people with a certain kind of mind. I, for example, have a very spiralling, out-of-control, soft-edged kind of mind. Given a subject, I can expand on it unto the ends of the universe. Starting with knitted dishrags, I can encompass Sumo wrestlers, Moroccan nights, yurts in Mongolia... For this reason, providing myself with a framework, gives my poem, my essay and my day structure and boundaries that help me focus on the matter at hand. Giving your work a decided framework may help you also, if you share my kind of mind.

So before beginning to write, make decisions on an outline or framework for your piece. You will discover that it invites content to rush into its proper place. In fiction, the questions of how many subplots, characters, dead bodies, intertwining couples, etc., would influence the decision of what the framework should be. For people like me, and in fact for many older writers, drawing up the framework is aided by using lists and lists start to become essential. You, as older writers, who have spent your lives running offices and factories, organizing families or sports teams, have a lifetime of experience in schedules and list-making that can be put to good service in whatever type of writing you choose. As far as poetry goes, so much of it is list-making anyway, and that comes very easily to anyone who has efficiently organized anything, let alone 60 years or more of life.

If your writing is not ordered and clear, the reader will not understand what you are writing about, even though it is very important to you. My rule is that I want to know who is doing what to whom, in what sequence and where it is all taking place. Frameworks help provide the clarity needed for effective writing.

For those of you who are of a more linear nature, however, and for whom giving your writing a structure is natural, consider brainstorming. Diagrams that stretch over on to the next page or jump outside the square and brain-loosening writing exercises are the things that will stretch your mind outside your clever organization. These may help you introduce fresh and surprising elements into your writing.

On writer's block

Now we come to the awkward moment when it's not the choice of form or framework that is the problem, but the fact that you have nothing forthcoming to hang on it. The dreaded moment of "will I ever write again?" – writer's block. In writer's block the material goes dead on you, and instead of carrying you along with its own intrinsic energy, it stops inviting you to take it further.

You would think after 60, or 70 years of restraint, your writing would flow endlessly, but no, this doesn't always happen. At such times, H. G. Wells recommended, "If you are in difficulties with a book, try the element of surprise: attack it at an hour when it isn't expecting it."

Here are some other ways of breaking writer's block that I have found effective:

- Work on more than one section of your writing at one time, so that if one area seems to have dried up, you can always turn to another.

- It occurred to me early on in my writing that when I came up against a block, it was because I might not have the writing skill to know how to handle it. Not knowing what else to do, I blasted my way through, that is, wrote a fair amount of rubbish until I came to an area that I once more felt comfortable with and so could continue. The rubble (and rubbish) I cleared up later when re-writing.

- Turn to a different kind of activity. I have my studio area set out like stations in a kindergarten classroom – writing, painting, fabric work, piano, reading chair and garden. When one area feels blocked, or completed, I just move over to another. Often a physical activity, where the body is moved in different ways, leaves the mind free so it can take its time to sort things out for you.

- Ride it light. Don't be pompous about your work. I recommend at least once a week that you stand in front of the bathroom mirror and see yourself as a clown, and laugh. Don't take yourself and your writing too seriously. If you stay blocked take up watercolour painting. I strongly recommend it.

- Like the milkmaid who is projecting too far ahead, calculating what she will buy with the money she will raise in town with her eggs and butter, and accidentally kicks the pail over so that her plans come to naught, writers also can be sidetracked. Plans for fame and fortune can beguile them so that they forget that there are decisions to be made in the material they are dealing with right now. Avoiding decision-making often leads to writer's block.

- Vanessa Grant claims each writer has their own natural writing pattern, so when her words stop, she doesn't panic, but relaxes, knowing they will soon start again. And so will yours.

Hemingway, he of the numerous rewrites, suggests "leaving a little water in the well," that is, at the end of a day's writing, leave a few notes as to how you want to continue...a few words written on the next page for you to pick up on the next day.

Generally, at the time of writer's block, the child in me emerges, but instead of lying on the floor and having a temper tantrum, I do what all good parents do when they want a child to do something. Forbid them to do it. To this end, I send myself off to do a vigorous, messy chore. As I progress with the chore, I start to feel how much I would prefer to be writing. I do not leave, however, and, if necessary, I extend the chosen chore. By this time I have a load of ideas piling up in my head and when, exhausted, I allow that my chore is complete, I find myself dashing to the machine with any block totally forgotten. By playing both the child and the mother (a little schizoid, I must admit), I trick myself into getting into the flow once more.

On editing in general

Once the writing is flowing and your work is completed (you think), it is time to call for your editing hat. For it is firm editing, rewriting and rewriting that will polish your piece. After all, Samuel Johnson reasonably points out, "What is written without effort is in general read without pleasure."

Writers' manuscripts are messy. We all know that...or do we? As Joan Bolker said, "I nearly fainted at Harvard's Houghton Library the first time I saw Keat's crossed out words in the manuscript "To Autumn," shocked by the thought the poem hadn't sprung complete and perfect from his pen."

If Hemingway rewrote the end of *A Farewell to Arms* thirty-nine times before he was satisfied, surely you can offer a dozen versions of that clumsy line or inappropriate metaphor. But write first, edit later. That is, get it all down as spontaneously as possible. If you edit as you go along, you may never finish a paragraph or a verse. Now that your floodgates have opened, get those fingers moving as rapidly as your ideas. Editing will follow in due course.

When you have placed the final full stop, Donna Levin recommends that you do one more draft than you think you can stand and then later, admitting she was wrong, she recommends two more drafts than you think you can stand. Bernard Malamud put it gently when he said, "First drafts are for learning what your novel or story is about."

Everyone has to do many drafts of their work to make sure the manuscript flows well and that what you have wanted to convey is clearly conveyed. This doesn't cover the many small mistakes that didn't get caught – repetition of words, phrases, even whole incidents, not to mention copy-editing errors such as spelling and punctuation that will make you cringe no matter how splendid the rest of the work is. You may just have to accept that a few mistakes and a few awkward patches will get through, no matter how many times you, and others, edit your piece. Recently, my husband read a brilliant book on intelligence. On the copyright page, the subject matter was listed as neurology, education and brian! I myself, on the back-cover of one of my books (the worst place to do it) misspelled "breathe." Nobody caught it, but I still blushed every time I saw it until it was corrected in the second print run.

If you are doing the editing of your writing yourself, don't edit more than two hours at a time – your eyes will be dimmed out by that time, never mind your brain. I use a computer for editing, but also have a hard copy beside me, because apparently I can catch mistakes more easily with my head bent down to a page than with my head raised to a screen.

Be gentle – reflections on editing poetry

As a person who has coached other writers and edited their poetry for some years, perhaps some musings on editing poetry will help you when you come to edit your own, if that is the form you have chosen for your writing. I apply the same principles I use for editing when I am reading poetry for pleasure. I must admit that I usually read with a sharp pencil stuck behind my ear.

The first poem I was ever asked to edit ran, if I can remember rightly, something like this:

> **I sit drinking**
> **my morning coffee.**
> **A cyclist rides by**
> **and disappears.**
> **An eagle flies past**
> **and does not return.**
> **Even the neighbour's dog**
> **trots into the distance.**
> **I take another sip.**

"Not satisfactory," I thought immediately. Then added to myself, "But what a great idea! He's writing about how all things come into being and pass away...the dog, the cyclist, the eagle...the transitoriness of it all! Just what I like expressing in my own writing." I began to wax eloquent over this truly profound idea that I had extracted from his poem and decided to show the writer, the writer who had requested a little help with it, how the poem should really be written.

I opened my computer and pounded out the following version:

**between one sip and another
the cyclist passes,
the eagle disappears
into the horizon,
and even the neighbour's dog
sniffs his way out of view
I take another sip**

No need for capitals and periods, that would imply a beginning and an ending, and I wanted this to be a perpetual poem. I sighed. It was by no means perfect, but so much deeper, more mysterious, more significant than his effort. It's true I had rewritten his whole poem, but then…I pressed SEND.

Wrapped up in my cleverness, I was startled to receive an indignant reply indicating that he had not meant anything like that at all, but was merely commenting on the many things one can see during a leisurely breakfast. Nor did he like my absence of capitals and punctuation – "very unconventional," he stated firmly. I stepped back (metaphorically) from his comments and realized I had broken the two most basic rules of editing someone else's poetry (or any other form of writing come to that).

1) Be clear what the writer is trying to say and allow him/her to say it.

2) Respect the way writers express themselves, their *modus operandi*.

But how to read a poet clearly? Firstly, I believe, poetry editors should read lots of poetry, become familiar with styles such as: emotive poetry, factual poetry, philosophical poetry, sensual poetry. Read poetry until it is flowing through your blood. As Mark Strand so beautifully says in his poem "Eating Poetry":

> **Ink runs from the corners of my mouth.**
> **There is no happiness like mine.**
> **I have been eating poetry.**

Then familiarize yourself with the variety of ways the great themes of life – birth, courtship, marriage, aging, death, love and strife – have been expressed in these poems you have been exploring.

They say that a person can only truly understand someone from his or her own culture, background and interests. That would mean that the wider the poetry editor's interests are, the more easily he/she will be able to reach out to help other poets. The deeper the editor understands human nature, and particularly their own nature, the more diverse the group of poets they can respond to with empathy. For empathy is what one needs when one is editing. Being able to see clearly what the poet is trying to say, without getting lost in the poet's emotions (or indeed in your own) is necessary.

As to the second rule – respect for the way a poet has chosen to express themselves – this could be sonnet, blank verse, haiku, ballad, ode, rhymed lines, short lines, long lines, satire, narrative. The list is lengthy.

Recently I edited a poet who loved short lines and long poems. Of course, the short lines increased the length of the poems and they stretched on for many pages. This was tiresome to the eye and to the fingers turning the pages. Moreover the ideas she wished to express seemed spread thin, and were hard to hold on to as one page moved into another. A one-page poem of short lines can suggest movement and often wit, but many pages...

By now I had learned the rules, and so put it gently to the poet that her very attractive ideas might be better portrayed in verse of longer lines thus capturing each of her thoughts in its own gem-like setting of, say, half a page. She found this recommendation appealing and it became almost a game for her to break the whole poem up into ideas, one per verse and to make each verse fit half a page. The final draft was on three pages (instead of seven) and had a strong visual appeal. We were both happy with it.

So if you are submitting poetry, or any other form of writing, to a publisher and it is suggested that you take a second look at your work, when working with an editor, consider carefully what is being advised. Don't cling to every word stubbornly, but trust that the editor will help you present a body of well-conceived and well-finished poems. That is their job and they can, more often than not, do it.

Late Bloomer: On Writing Later in Life

My most recent editing work spanned nine months, and at some moment towards the end of that period, I realized a poet had been born. This first-time writer (in her 50s) worked extremely hard and was willing to produce that extra draft until she felt absolutely satisfied. Well maybe not absolutely satisfied, since most writers are discontented with their work and it has to be snatched away from them to stop their last-minute tinkering. But on the other hand, as X.J. Kennedy says, "The world is full of poets with languid wrenches who don't bother to take the last six turns on their bolts." It is the function of poetry editors to be there with the poets to help those last six rotations.

Here are some guidelines for you poets for when you are considering the poem you have just written:

1) Did it say what you wanted it to say?

2) Is it true and ethical, does it have integrity, etc.?

3) Does it meander off your theme?

4) Is it smug?

5) Is it riddled with clichés?

6) Is it finished?

If you are dissatisfied with your work here are some things you might try:

1) Close your writing book, computer, or whatever, and rewrite the poem from heart. See what differences have appeared. Which do you like better?

2) Change from first person to third, or vice versa.

3) Check for clichéd metaphors and similes – drowning in tears, etc.

4) Perform surgery – cut, cut, cut.

5) Take one image or metaphor and make a new poem out of it.

6) Set the poem aside in a file marked in progress.

Some people maintain that you should keep every scrap you have ever written. I am not of that school. It's up to you whether you file away every word you've ever written as if it were a diamond. I don't bother if the poem is not coming together, or if the book turns out to be a bad idea even though I'm half way through writing it. I don't expect a click every time and have thrown away several books without an ounce of regret (although I must admit I've sometimes got a good poem or even a haiku from the discard before it went into the wastebasket). This does seem like the ultimate edit, but trust that if there was a good idea in the work, it will come back in a more useable form later.

6 *Finding support and encouragement*

Workshops and classes

I have been giving writing workshops for some time now and, although I've been curious, I've never had the temerity to ask my students why they sign up. I, myself, take a class from another writer to fill a specific area in which I feel weak, such as dialogue, to learn about a wider variety of poetic forms, or to learn how to write in public areas unselfconsciously.

I am, on the whole, a poor student. I tend to clown around in class, do not pay full attention, misunderstand, and so do the exercises incorrectly, or, about turn, and go way beyond what the poor teacher has asked us to write. Even as a child I tended to under- or over-perform; in retrospect, I suppose I was a contrary child who never gave a teacher exactly what she or he demanded. I can remember once being given an assignment and writing forty pages on camouflage in the animal kingdom, which my teacher had to at least pretend to plough through. I suppose these days, with Google for research, I could have run that to two hundred pages. Teachers tend not to want me in their workshops.

If I really want to consult someone on some aspect of writing, one-on-one works better for me. After I get over the idea that I'm being self-indulgent, I can usually get the teacher to focus on the specific problem I want to work on. The fee is well worth it. Sometimes, as a bonus, the clever teacher gives me the lesson I really need to learn, and I am humble enough to take it. For example I had a one-on-one session with a teacher who specializes in editing film scripts. I wanted her to give me clues for writing good dialogue, whereas she taught me how to build on my strength, which I discovered was the ability to link disconnected subjects. She did this by the simple exercise of asking me to choose two objects at random in my kitchen (the best teaching is done at kitchen tables) and then write a dialogue between the two. Ostensibly I was doing dialogue, in reality I was linking the disparate. Clever teacher!

My advice about workshops is not to become a workshop groupie. In the flush of your amazing production at your first workshop (Why not? You have been waiting 60 years to let go.) you sign up for "creative writing," "finding your true voice," "the writer within," "the writer without." Oh, the list is endless. You may learn something at each workshop, but the odds are you would be better served locked in the basement with your computer and a week's supply of food and drink.

Too many workshops can (instead of encouraging experimentation) be inhibiting. You can become too schooled and mannered (following rules doesn't make for good writing). Or, on the other hand, you can become totally confused by the many different approaches taken by the teachers.

Some say, cynically, that workshop-givers wouldn't be doing it if their work sold, but few writers can actually support themselves by writing alone (not to mention if the chosen form is poetry). So be charitable towards, and respectful of, workshop-givers. Most of them work hard at making their workshops upbeat and productive. There is always the danger, however, of teachers repeating the same material time and time again so that they doze off (as do their attendees), bored by their own laziness. *Prenez-garde!*

Recently, I have been giving a workshop for Late Bloomers, for people who, maybe like yourself, have been saying for a long while that they would write one day, but haven't started yet. The workshop is a one-time jump-start, kick-in-the-pants workshop where I keep the attendees writing at a ferocious pace. I start without any introductions, go-arounds of where they are at, or other pleasantries. I want to cut out their intellects, their self-consciousness and the little consciences that sit on their shoulders telling them what they can and cannot do.

The way I do it is by giving clear instructions for each exercise and then letting them loose, keeping their pens, or pencils, moving all the while. Lest their eccentricities and egos pop into the session and spoil it all, I barely give the participants time to finish an exercise and do a voluntary read-out-loud of what they have written, before I begin the next exercise. I have assumed that the people who come to my workshops can write, and this notion is so firmly fixed in my mind (whether it is true, or not) that they have no alternative but to write, and write they do.

After a workshop such as this, the budding writer can settle down to work with someone who can take them through the mechanics of writing on specifics such as journalistic writing, or writing true romances, and they are well away. Often the attendees of my workshops bond strongly in the short but intense period we are all together and they keep in contact later. Sometimes they form support groups with no facilitator present at all.

Helping each other – support groups

Writers don't really want advice, they want support.

During my first marriage I devoted myself to husband and children, yet dissatisfaction wore my edges frayed. My creative energies didn't seem to get fully expressed by only making meals and supporting others (though they could have, had I been more aware). One day my bewildered first husband, an artist, not knowing what to do with my irritability, gave me a large piece of beautiful drawing paper. I was aghast and sat with pencil poised over it for some time. Eventually

I drew a very small square right in the middle, and that was all I did, no matter how much I was encouraged. My creativity was a tiny box that was waiting to explode. Don't shut yours into a similar small space.

As human beings, Trungpa Rinpoche stated, "We must continue to open in the face of tremendous opposition. No one is encouraging us to open and still we must peel away the layers of the heart." Good advice both for life and for writing. Still, we can't all rush to Tibetan teachers for support. Where can writers go to get support for opening that small box, peeling those onion layers, or taking the safety deposit out of their creative bank?

The usual place to turn first, when it comes to sharing your writing, is to your family. Family often offers a warm but critical ear. If family isn't available (or is even hostile to and threatened by your creative efforts), turn to friends. You have chosen them over the years for their support in other ways, now try them on your manuscripts. If your friends are not as sensitive to your literary efforts as you would like, a writing group may be the answer for support and encouragement. A group of writers, preferably in different fields, who can listen, give input, connect you up with others, give advice on publishing and encourage you to come back month after month is often the best thing to have. They can be trusted to watch caringly as you take your first tentative steps, stumble a bit, tear away at an incredible speed, stop dead for weeks on end, or steadily produce year after year.

Here are Margot Finke's comments on her writers' group, "The speedy passing of years shocked me into doing something pragmatic and sensible. I formed a critique group. Writing is a lonely occupation. My group encouraged and comforted me. They inspired me to write stronger plots and create richer characters. My paragraphs of fluff were pruned." [www.underdown.org/mf-late_blooming.htm]

But not everyone considers writing groups to be the answer, for sharing what you are writing may spoil its freshness. After all, it is said that the best cooking is done by keeping the lid firmly on the pot until it's finished. It's the intensity created between you and the page that produces the purest writing. As Andrew Wyeth also so succinctly warns, "When you show it to someone, if they like it, you're stopped, and if they dislike it, you're stopped either way."

For those of you who might appreciate knowing what to look for in a good writing group, here's what you should be watching for:

• A strong aim for the group, for example, to produce a small magazine, or chapbook.

• Rules, but flexible ones – everyone should try to bring a new piece of writing to each meeting, but doesn't have to.

• Tea and cookies should not be conspicuous (you can gossip just as well at home).

- No ranking of forms of writing – such as the ranking of SF, true romances and limericks as fairly low on the totem pole, when they are just as valid as creative efforts as philosophical, or erudite writing.

- A few folks shouldn't dominate the meetings.

- Critiquing should be constructive, not shattering.

- Ideas can be shared, but other's original themes should be respected, not adopted.

- You should leave the meeting elated and strengthened in the worth of your own writing.

For a short period I attended a writer's support group. The folks were all good people, earnest and decent. So decent that nobody wanted to offer any criticism and, in fact, praise was also absent (perhaps being considered a possible source of hubris). I started to write a number of depressing poems on death, in order to try for some kind of reaction, but everyone continued to smile benignly. Eventually I tore out my guts and wrote a poem "On Being Thought a Jew" – a subject rather central to my life. I could have been reciting a verse on seaweed! I decided to cut my losses and made that meeting the last day of my attendance.

A new member had arrived on that ill-fated evening. He read avidly from a thick mass of papers. It was the first chapter of a horror story. It was revolting, horrendous and completely captivating. I heard via the island grapevine that he continued to regale the group for a year after my departure, despite their exclamations of regret at his savage approach to life. At least he got a reaction and I got a strange kind of remote satisfaction.

Support doesn't have to be just literary. Practical support is wonderful too – someone to pay your mortgage, cook your meals, clean your house, trim your garden. My husband, the sculptor Elias Wakan, and I decided that we both needed just such a person. As this did not seem likely to happen, we decided to split the chores down the middle and now we are both able to tap away on the keys or sculpt (though not at the same time, of course) while the sounds of lawn mower, delicious smells from the kitchen, hammering repairs to the porch and sounds of soothing music are provided by a supportive partner.

If your partner, parents, siblings, offspring are not supportive, the obvious suggestion is to find new ones. If this action strikes you as a bit drastic, at least find substitutes. As I suggested above, friends, writing classes, writers' groups may give you enough support to carry on. Goodness knows writing is a difficult enough aim even with a fully supportive environment around you.

However, if none other is available, you must learn to trust yourself:

> Take a pen in your uncertain fingers.
> Trust, and be assured
> That the whole world is a sky-blue butterfly
> And words are the nets to capture it

> *– Muhammad al-Ghuzzi "The Pen",*
> *trans. May Jayyusi and*
> *John Heath-Stubbs*

A little more on criticism and feedback

I know a very dear, good man...thoughtful and caring of the world's woes, who sends out a regular newsletter of his views. It is pompous, deadly boring and wouldn't encourage anyone to any kind of action except perhaps that of deleting his newsletter from your e-mail. Another friend, for a birthday present, paid for a professional editor to edit some of our mutual friend's material. The results (which we agreed with completely) were devastating to our dear friend.

Age can make you indifferent to criticism, or can make you even more vulnerable to the slightest negative appraisal. However, if you want to see your material in print, unless you self-publish, you will have to learn to take criticism. You can find a positive reaction to your writing if you select your critic carefully enough. On the whole though, it is better to start by feeling good about your writing in your own estimate. Then two understandings will help you a lot. The first is that one should realise that your writing could be improved by intelligent editing. Often new writers are devastated if a word of their efforts is changed – that is nonsense! A good professional editor knows if the writing just doesn't work, and you should learn to do that too. The second understanding is that your writing may not be to everybody's taste. Grasping these two facts will help you to keep things in good perspective and will save you a certain amount of mental anguish when the rejections start pouring in.

Sometimes when you ask for criticism you don't really want it. Maybe you just want praise and maybe you just want to talk it over with someone for, as you talk, things often get clearer. Be certain as to what you really want when you ask for feedback. My friend whom I mentioned above, he of the heavy, political e-mails, was not really asking for feedback, either literary or political, when he dispersed his electronic essays. He was looking for a platform for his views. His friends misunderstood, and thought he was asking for a critiquing of his literary style, suggestions for getting his message across more palatably. He was not, and there lay the pain and confusion, both for us and for him.

One way of controlling the criticism, if control it you must, is to mark the passages/verses you are satisfied with and just ask for criticism of the ones that seem incomplete. Simply tell the critic just how much feedback you want. Or try reading your writing aloud. You'll immediately see the flaws, the boring bits and the rough bits. Often when reading in public, I want to stop and change the manuscript at the points where my reading falters. These awkward parts that jar are what you need a critic for.

Also ask your critics to look out for quirks in style and mannerisms you may just not be aware of – over-use of commas, over-use of some phrase. I find myself using "of course" and "however" far too many times.

If you want feedback, don't argue – listen! It is hard for we older writers to take advice from younger ones. We think we have been around a block or two and that our life experience counts for something. Yes it does, but when it comes to editing and critiquing you should want and accept an expert opinion, irrespective of age. Age has nothing to do with the skill of getting to the root of the awkward paragraph or incoherent theme.

Pay for your feedback with money if a professional is doing it; don't expect something for nothing, or that is what you'll get. Send a thank you and a small gift for selected critiquing by a friend, or be more generous by writing an acknowledgment of their help in the book, or even by giving them a dedication, if the help has been overwhelming. If you have selected your editor carefully, you will be well rewarded. Although you need an editor who is sympathetic to your style of writing and one that hears your voice, don't seek out too many. Settle for one whose opinions you respect enough to listen to, and stay with him or her. A variety of conflicting advice will confuse you.

There is only so much advice you can take without losing your own hard-won voice.

Remember praise doesn't last. If you want more applause (and it is addictive) keep writing and keep writing well.

7 What to do when the work is finished

> *"It's as hard to get from almost finished to finished as to get from beginning to almost done."*
> – Elinor Fuchs

You can't, however, publish your manuscript until it is finished. For me, finishing a book has two aspects. The first is actually drawing the book to a conclusion, an ending, either happy, unhappy, or maybe suspended so that a sequel is possible. The second is what I call fidgeting and authors are terrible fidgets. They return to early chapters and tinker with them, add tension to the middle section, or fuss with the last words. All this may be justified, but it may also be procrastination, for the strange procrastination that prevents a writer from starting on a book is also present at the book's conclusion. The writer just doesn't want to let go. But let go they must if they ever w\ant to see the book in print and start on a new story, a new book.

If your aim is to start writing and no more (and that is certainly a good and sufficient aim), then keep your written pieces, finished or not, in their respective files on the machine and back them up onto a CD. Mark the CD with the titles of the pieces you have saved on it. You should also print out a hard copy, put it in a manilla file and place it in your desk drawer. That way it will all be there should you decide later on that you might like to see some of your work in print. If you want your friends, offspring and grandchildren to see what you have been writing, run off copies for them.

If you have the money and want your efforts to be printed immediately, have the manuscript laid out by a competent desktop publisher and printed hard or soft cover on archival paper. If money is no object, have the hardcover bound in leather and the cover printed in gold leaf. Even if you can afford to self-publish, I recommend that you don't rely on self-editing and that you get a proof reader to run through the manuscript before it goes to press. Mistakes, missed in the editing, seem to be printed in bold when the author reads his or her printed book. I know from experience.

If you'd like to embark on the writer's life, however, and want to see your work in print in magazines, newspapers and eventually books put out by publishers, start sending your manuscripts out to suitable small magazines or local newspapers. Be satisfied with no payment beside your byline or tear sheets at first, or, if your work has gone into an anthology, one copy of the book.

Yes, you do hear of a few authors getting huge advances (on their royalties) and being booked into wonderful venues for their book launches. Occasionally this happens, but more realistically, imagine no advance on royalties and just a few venues booked for your book launch or reading tour, – mostly shopping malls and local libraries where folk, who have come in to keep out of the weather, cluster around to hear what you have to say. If you keep these images firmly in mind, anything more will be a pleasant surprise.

If you're very anxious to get printed, you may get caught in a process that is not really illegal, but is considered vanity by most professional writers. A person advertises for material, asks for a fee for reading it and, if it goes into a book (which it usually does) makes you sign the dotted line to buy five copies at $25 each. The book does arrive and your writing will certainly be in it, but...

New Year's Resolution

**Never mind how fine
your fine journal is,
I have vowed this year
to write for no journal
that pays in copies
(whether one, or two).
I also promise to submit my work
to no competitions.
My principles?
Good poems cannot be graded
and are worth at least
a buck or two.**

Naomi Beth Wakan

Here's an aside about the so-called vanity press. In years gone by, paying to have your own work published was not unknown. Several famous writers have financed their own printings, including William Blake, Virginia Woolf, Walt Whitman and William Morris. Irma von Starkloff Rombauer self-published her cook book, *The Joy of Cooking,* which went on to sell more than 14 million copies and is still selling. More recently, however, it has been considered a form of vanity to pay for your own work to appear in print. It was considered a little unseemly that you had not gone through the rigorous process of submitting your manuscript to publishers and experiencing a demanding period of editing, should it be accepted. By the time your manuscript saw publication you had, so to speak, run the gauntlet of what was expected of a writer who wished to be considered serious.

Today, with the skills of desktop publishing so readily available, many writers find they don't have to go through the paces listed above. No one thinks the worse of them for choosing to get the book out speedily themselves, rather than wait the average two years between submission and publication at an established publisher. Self-published writers are, however, usually stuck with a pile of books in their basement, having forgotten that books, besides needing writing and publishing, also need distributing and selling.

The Internet also offers many new possibilities for getting your writings out speedily to the public eye. I did a series on popular children's literature writers for a web-magazine. I'm afraid I ignored the rules and advice for successful

Internet writing, but got paid well for my old-style hard copy writing behaviour. For those of you who are anxious to seize your chances with the slew of e-zines that are springing up, you might like to start with advice from some of the sites below and go from there. Please remember that web sites open and close more speedily than restaurants, and so some sites in the list may not have survived by the time you read this book:

www.businessknowhow.com/Writers/freelance

www.webreference.com/internet/writing

www.askoxford.com/betterwriting/osa/internet

www.internetbasedmoms.com/writing-internet/
internet-writingrules

As I said, writers usually start by submitting material to small modest outlets, whether in print, on-line e-zines or local newspapers. Which are your favourite magazines or newspapers? And in the magazines, or newspapers that you read, which are your favourite sections, favourite columnists? The ones you choose will tend to reflect the kind of writing you like best, perhaps the kind of writing you wish you were doing yourself. At my Late Bloomer workshops, I ask the attendees to speak briefly on their favourite magazine or journal. They almost always, in their description of why they like it so much, will give a reason that defines how they would like their own writing to be. The danger is to go on reading those magazines forever, somehow confusing the magazine's writers' efforts with your own, as you recline on the couch admiring them. Reading Zen books doesn't make you enlightened and reading fine writers is all very well...but you are a fine writer too; where is your writing?

When you have a few magazine, or newspaper acceptances to your credit, you are now ready to approach a book publisher. Again make it a modest choice.

Submission, and mainly rejection

No matter how old we are, do we ever accept rejection with good grace? Rejection is what happens to writers (older or younger) who submit material. It is a perfectly natural process like old age and death – dreaded and yet to be expected. At least that's what I keep reassuring myself as if, somehow, by learning to deal creatively and gracefully with rejection, I can also respond similarly to sickness, old age and death.

If I don't submit work, I won't get rejected, that's for sure; but I also won't have that slim chance of getting accepted either. The saying goes submit in haste, be rejected at leisure, and that seems to fit me very well. I will toy with a manuscript for weeks, often months, then one day, for no reason that I can discern, I'll quickly print it out, add a casual, often witty (might as well enjoy the process) cover letter and a self-addressed, stamped envelope, and off it goes.

The least offensive rejection letters I get usually start with an apology. "We're so sorry we took so long responding to your submission." (One year after submission.) "Sorry not to have better news," or, not wasting any time, "Unfortunately I am unable to find a place for it on our list." They may slip in a few compliments – "your book is deserving of publication," and a few words of warning, "the language was unnecessarily elaborate," "the narrator was focused on a little too much," or, "I thought this quite cute but a bit too preachy for my taste."

Then there is the dreaded form rejection:

```
We are returning your manuscript because:

✈ It's not suited to our present needs.
❑ Its language or concept is too mature
  for our audience.
❑ We seldom buy rhyming picture books.
❑ It needs more character/plot development.
❑ We have a very limited non-fiction line.

                          Sincerely,
                          The Editors
```

Well at least I know my language is not too mature but that, yet once more, I've just guessed their needs wrongly.

I do that a lot. Most of it comes from my fine powers of visualization that are so acute that they can see my manuscript firmly in print in the magazine to which I have chosen to submit. I can do this so well that I usually miss their fine script – "we only accept manuscripts in October and February," or "we only accept manuscripts from agents," or, worse yet, illustrating my complete lack of attention to the state of the journal, "we regret to announce we have ceased publication."

And yet, and yet…I have had sentimental pieces published in hard-boiled literary magazines and my expoundings on haiku have appeared in garden magazines, so sometimes a little carelessness pays off. Publishers, I know, hate writers who spray their submissions out like a garden-sprinkler gone berserk, but some days, that's just how I want to do it.

Since one never wants to play tennis with anyone less skilled than oneself, I make it a practice to submit to magazines that are slightly more intellectual or more humanistic than is my day-to-day performance, or to journals that have a slightly broader circulation than my writing deserves. Might as well lever oneself up a little each submission. But be careful of levering yourself up too high. An attendee at one of my workshops waxed indignant that her first efforts, sent to *Reader's Digest* and *The New Yorker* magazine (without a self-addressed stamped envelope) had not even been acknowledged, let alone accepted. Leave these magazines alone until later…much later.

These days, with a large mortgage to pay, I usually Post-it® (am I the first to use this trademark as a verb?) the pages of *Writer's Market* according to the dollar sign attached to the publisher's information. $ indicates 10 cents or less per word, $$ = 10-50 cents per word, $$$ = 50 cents to one dollar a word, you get the idea. Gone are my salad days when thought of publication in a little magazine with the added inducement of pay in copies was infinitely attractive. Though not a gambler, I have started to consider the odds. I do it this way. In *Writer's Market* and books of that ilk, you will often see recorded how many submissions the firm receives a year, and how many books they publish. By dividing one by the other you get clear odds of your chance of acceptance. This is a good rough guide, unless, of course, you have a totally exclusive, brilliant topic that only you can write about.

A mature writer, I am told, accepts rejection and criticism, so once I have got over my ranting, raving and crying, I reread the rejection comments and find, to my surprise, that they were often true and usually helpful. So, if the editor says, "try us again", I cheer up, take them literally and do so. Editors are busy people and even these three little words take time to write. An editor wouldn't waste them if they didn't mean them is how I reason.

William Zinsser says of rejection, "I don't shake my fist at the editor for not recognizing the jewel he was offered.

I type a new covering letter and get my article back in the mailbox by noon." Now that's how mature writers behave.

My favourite rejection was the one Gertrude Stein's editor, A.J. Fifield, sent to her: "Being only one, having only one pair of eyes, having only one time, having only one life, I cannot read your MS three or four times. Not even one time. Only one look is enough. Hardly one copy would sell. Hardly one. Hardly one."

I consider some of my writing to come from a place that I don't know about; the writing surprises me, and it is that writing that I respect. I have learned over the years though, that my own estimation of it doesn't have to be equally respected by others. However, I do not, as Nancy Mairs states, feel spurned, degraded, hollowed out and tossed aside when I receive a rejection letter. I don't tear them up, but place them in a file as material for a witty piece I will write some time down the road.

Certainly the first sight of your name under a piece of writing is exhilarating. J.M.Barrie was more than exhilarated with his first book, "For several days after my first book was published I carried it about in my pocket, and took surreptitious peeks at it to make sure the ink had not faded."

I felt that way also when I saw a copy of my first hardcover book from a large children's publisher. But I also remembered the years of pleasure I had had writing aimlessly with no thought of submission of the material, and certainly no contract in sight. So being published is not the end of the story, nor should it even be the beginning. Writing is a creative process sufficient to itself and if the poems/essays/articles/novels never see the light of day outside your desk drawer that is fine, if that is what you want. Concentrating on money and fame is harmful, and I mean very harmful, to good writing.

Do not write poems

**Do not write poems
of brilliant clarity
else they will enable
you to dine with kings
and mix with members
of the government.
Soon the Mafia
will be surrounding
and protecting you,
and the paparazzi
will encounter you
at breakfast…and
you'll never be able
to write a poem
of brilliant clarity
again.**

Naomi Beth Wakan

Unless you are trying to tell yourself (and you alone) something in a private diary, or in a therapeutic journal, writing is usually viewed as a form of communication – not that communicating with yourself isn't a first necessary step. Still, you will probably eventually want to at least read your efforts to your family, your writers' group, try it out on your book club members or see that it is inserted somewhere in your community newspaper. We Late Bloomers have a certain urgency when it comes to communication, I think, and perhaps a certain obligation to fully show ourselves (or at least our best profile) before it is too late.

Bon voyage and good luck.

PART 2

Interviews

The toll of years: an interview with myself

In Part 2 of *Late Bloomer* I am going to introduce you to a number of people, just like yourself, who wanted to write for many years and didn't start until the later part of their lives. They range from folks who have tried a few first, hesitant haiku, to people recording a memoir, to others who have launched on a full autobiography, to yet others who have had a first story or poem published and some who are well-established writers. I have always admired doctors who tried out their cures on themselves first, so I think I'd better start by asking myself the questions that I have asked my interviewees.

1) *What made you start writing in your later years?*

A mortgage and an interest in sharing my experience of living in Japan with school children studying Japan on their Grade 6 curriculum in British Columbia

2) *How did you find your voice?*

By finding myself as a human being – through meditation, healing, music, dance and gardening. The voice began to appear when I was about 40, but didn't gain reasonable consciousness until I was in my 60s. I just knew I had found it because there seemed to be no separation between myself and the page...difficult to describe, but my everyday self appeared to have stepped aside and just let the writing write itself.

3) *What form did you choose to express yourself in?*

To earn a living, I wrote educational material. To stay in the present, I wrote haiku.

4) *Did the process of writing change the way you think about yourself?*

Yes. As I expressed my true self, I gained a confidence in my abilities (and learned their limits) as well as knowing that I could write with an integrity that readers felt was disarming.

5) *What did you/are you doing with the material you have written?*

I have written children's educational material, a children's fiction book, two books on haiku, a book of longer poems, gathered material and contributed small poems for 10 books of quotations (with my twin sister) and produced a book on how to write memoirs.

6) *What are the positives and negatives of writing as an older person?*

I'm afraid my answer to this question is rather meandering and lengthy and so I would like to put it in essay form:

Chapter 8: The toll of years: an interview with myself

"[You] Don't know how people look through you. Talk about you as if you weren't there. Smile politely when you make a remark." – quoted from an elderly lady in a detective story by Jeanne M. Dams

Yes! When I stand around alone at a party, I often find Jeanne Dam's observations ring true, until they find out that despite my grey hair, glasses perched at the end of my nose and slight stoop, I actually have a number of books under my belt. On the whole, though, the positives of coming to writing later in my life have more than compensated for the difficulties. If the balance didn't lean a little that way, I would have given up writing years ago.

Let's start with some definite disadvantages. The first being my noticeably shorter attention span, which makes sticking at the machine a real effort, instead of a delight. I only seem to be able to write in short, exhausting, intense bursts. At first I felt guilty about this new pattern, but as it seems to have arrived to stay, I have created strategies to harness these strong but momentary eruptions of energy. I alternate shorter writing periods with musing on my next poem while lying in a lounge chair, practicing my Grade 5 level piano skills, preparing food or reading a chapter in a good book. If I am interviewing others or listening to something I need to know, I make sure I am taking notes and fixing my full attention on the matter. When I am disinterested, my eyes tend to wander, which is disconcerting for the person I am with. I compensate for this by exaggerating my body position so that it faces them intensely and then I put a look of concerned and fascinated interest on my face. Sometimes this matches how I feel and sometimes not. I am very aware that this ability to concentrate is taking more effort than it used to.

My memory is changing as well. I can remember my father making a mosaic back-step into the garden 64 years ago better than I can remember where we are supposed to be going this weekend. To combat this tendency, I follow my own recommendation and have notebooks and pencils (well sharpened) in every room of the house, plus in the car and a flashlight beside the bed.

My short attention span seems to be accompanied by a mild irritation with the world around me. I have long ago resigned myself to reading distressing headlines in the paper everyday and try to level out this irritation by noting good things happening in my community and the many acts of kindness of friends. These small things keep me from feeling that the world is going completely insane. It is hard to keep writing if one feels depressed about mankind's future.

Physically sitting too long at the computer, at any age, produces sore backs and carpel-tunnel wrists. As I age, I become more self-protective and carry cushions for sitting on around with me, and foam pads for resting my wrists on are waiting on the desk. As I'm not into jogging, I keep myself in a shape that can at least write for an hour or two each day by alternating writing and wandering in the garden, or banging around the kitchen.

As I get older, my clothes get comfier and somewhat gaudier. I have been known to spit in the gutter, when other means of expectorating were not available. This behaviour does not directly affect my writing ability. I am, however, more inclined to tell people exactly what I think of them. I am getting less inhibited socially and less able to put up with what I feel is nonsense. This often makes for great poetry with true integrity, but sometimes I forget, and as Simon Armitage warns, "There's nothing like a punch in the mouth to remind you that that poem about your next-door neighbor was not as clever as you thought."

Lest this present an image of a crotchety, declining old woman, I should mention that age, for me, brings on a certain kind of detachment, with an ability to view matters from a greater distance and from many more view points. A basic calm exists under my surface irritation and best of all, I know that I am, more often than not, in touch with an essence that gives integrity to my writing.

Perhaps where my age shows the most is in a general slowing down. No longer do I shoot submissions out left, right and centre. No longer do I spray publishers with bright query letters. No longer do I keep membership up in groups that might further my career (their appeals pile up on my desk). No longer do I cultivate the right people who might nudge my fame along. In fact, ideas of career, fame and fortune have faded from my mind as I concentrate all my remaining creative energies on making a perfect poem or on encouraging others to do likewise.

Paradoxically enough, coming to terms with certain undeniable limitations of my physical and mental state has made pathways smoother and doors slightly more open. So, if you are fretting that it is too late! Just too late! Please don't. Just stay with the joy of whatever you are writing and let that be reward enough. Anything more will be icing on the cake.

Regrets, yes I regret that I didn't continue writing the small verses I started as a child. My stepsister had threatened to run off with a poet and that decided the family against encouraging any precocious writing skills that I might have displayed. Eli, my husband, pointed out just the other day that successful people seem to be those who knew from around the age of eight years old what they wanted to be when they grew up and then stayed with that goal. I was persuaded from the goal of being a writer and, in addition, I failed to grow up. All things considered, I haven't done too badly for someone who remembered and picked up their eight-year-old self's goal at age 60.

But the past can be blamed for everything, can't it? So when I find myself putting down my deficiencies to my birth as the second twin – two hours late and into the incubator – or blaming my card-playing parents for my lack of sophistication and worldly knowledge, I know its time to sit down at the computer and do some real writing. No one can be blamed for my procrastination.

I feel a small guilt when, as an older writer, I am not encouraging enough of beginning writers who seek me out for advice. I am well aware that the creative act of putting words on paper is a difficult one and I should be more generous with my praise. To that end I have started giving workshops for Late Bloomers like myself and love the hours I spend praising and encouraging them in every way I can think of. I may not get a Dostoevsky out of my workshops, but I get a lot of enthused feedback. I assume it is genuine and that I really have sent off the people who attend my workshops fired with fresh energy and supportive advice.

Henry James' remark, "It's better to have a success as a writer in mid-age rather than in youth because at least then when you're dropped by a fickle public, you have a life to go back to," has always amused me. But no, I don't intend to return to my earlier occupations partly because none of them seemed to have lasted longer than two years before I glazed over with boredom and partly because I am a person who never tries to return across a burned bridge.

However James' comment does make me consider the other positives of being a writer who started late in life.

• I have confidence, both with the writing task before me and with my ability to please an audience at my readings. My publisher said that I would wow any audience that didn't have body piercings and I have settled for that limitation.

- An ability to make mistakes without being overwhelmed at my incompetence.

- An ability to be criticized and rejected without taking it too personally.

- I have found it wonderful to be able to see life as almost an outsider, certainly to be able to see it from many perspectives and with a certain tolerance.

- It's great to have, if not a new career, at least a new absorption and one that can go in so many directions.

- Many writers point to the varied number of life-experiences an older writer has to draw on. As I have always lived in some parallel universe, even though I have travelled widely and changed occupations often, I still seem to rely on my little floating bubble of a world for most of my writing themes.

Now that I have shared where I'm at, I will turn to the experiences of other Late Bloomers. I know that their stories about beginning to write later in life will advise and enrich your own beginning as a writer.

9Mildred Tremblay

I count my own responses in with the thirteen writers I interviewed who started later in life, for I, too am a Late Bloomer. For the superstitious out there, it also rounds the writers interviewed off to an even fourteen. I'd now like to introduce you to the first of the writers that I interviewed.

I first heard of Mildred through a heated discussion about her uninhibited poetry at an art class I was attending. Intrigued, I read the book and then invited Mildred and other members of her writing group to read at a two-day poetry festival that I helped organize. She was everything I expected – feisty, strong and a fine reader. The fact that she was then in her early 90s only added to her distinctive personality.

Mildred Tremblay was born in Kenora, Ontario. After motherhood and years of working in her husband's company, she started writing. She very quickly established herself as a fine writer with great integrity. Her writing has won many awards including the League of Canadian Poets Annual Poetry Competition Award, *ARC* Magazine's Poem of the Year Contest Award, both awarded in 1996 and the Orillia

Humor Award, in 2000. In 2005, Mildred won the Vancouver International Writer's Festival Award for poetry. She has written a book of short fiction, *Dark Forms Gliding* in addition to her poetry. Her first collection of poetry, *Old Woman comes out of the Cave* was followed by another, *The Thing about Dying*. Both are from Oolichan Books.

Mildred well remembers the energy she had when she started writing: "I remember when I first started writing short stories in my early 50s, I spent months writing and revising and retyping a single story (and no computers then), I couldn't begin to do that now. That's one reason I switched to poetry – not that writing poetry is easier, it's not, but it's easier to handle smaller blocks of writing. I've no doubt that writers who are still young or middle-aged sit up all night writing sometimes. That's not possible at my age."

She adds a note perhaps true for writers at any age: "Intense long periods of writing have a peculiar sort of energy drain to them, different from other sorts of work – it's a very depleted sort of feeling, as if one has used up one's core."

Mildred feels one great advantage of starting to write as an older person is that "when you hit that time of life (early 50s, say), it is a great boost to find a new passion, the whole new fascinating boundless world of writing opening up for you; it certainly helps with the transition to becoming a senior." She adds, "Of course perhaps having more time and more financial freedom are other advantages."

Here are Mildred's responses to the survey questions:

Naomi: *What made you start writing in your later years?*

Mildred: Never in my wildest dreams did I think I could be a "writer." I had put my writing gift into writing letters to my sister and cousin. I wrote letters for years.

After I turned 50 I did a whole bunch of new things all at once. I quit smoking, I learned to drive, I took up meditation (a major path in my life) and I started to write.

My children were almost grown, although I still had a couple of teenagers. I was keeping books for a small company owned by my husband and myself – I was the office manager – but this didn't engage me passionately, as you can imagine.

I was sitting at the kitchen table mooning over a college catalogue in which "creative writing" was offered. Oh, if only, I thought, if only I was "good enough" to sign up for that. One of my daughters was there, and it was she who determined then and there that I would take the course. "You write most marvellous letters," she said, "you are a wonderful writer."

I resisted with every ounce of my being. Oh no, I couldn't do that, quite impossible, forget it. But she wouldn't take no for an answer. It was she who dragged me off by my coat collar, brought me to the college where we talked to the instructor, Kevin Roberts, about whether I had sufficient writing ability to take the class. My daughter kept saying: "Oh she's a marvellous writer," and I kept saying, "Oh no I'm not. I can't write."

She won. I registered for the class. And I'll tell you I never looked back. When I entered that room, and for the first time in my life met people who were interested in writing, talked about writing, practiced writing, it was as if the gates of paradise had opened for me. It was there I made some of my best friends I ever had and still have today. And it was there I found out not only that I could write, but that I was a gifted writer. It was the beginning of my second life.

Naomi: *How did you find your voice?*

Mildred: I had been writing traditionally for a short while when I read a book of stories by Michelle Tremblay (no relation) that was my introduction to magic realism. I was immediately hooked. I had a hundred stories in my head of that genre, and hadn't realized stories like that were not only publishable, but in demand. After that I began to read what was then called the "South American writers" – Gabriel Marquez being a major influence – and within a few years, a book of my stories was published under the title *Dark Forms Gliding.* After that I went on to poetry. It was with poetry that I began to seriously explore my Catholic childhood and women's lives. So I would say I found my voice by writing what I naturally liked to write.

Naomi: *In what form did you choose to express yourself?*

Mildred: The class I had registered for was studying short stories. So, that's where I started. I later went on to study poetry also.

Naomi: *Did the process of writing change the way you think about yourself, and, if so, how?*

Mildred: Yes, I began to think of myself as a "writer." I saw that I had the character of a writer, I was born to it, it was in my blood. All my life I had said: I am a reader, not a writer. I didn't realize that being a reader is a major characteristic of a writer.

Naomi: *What did you/are you doing with the material you have written?*

Mildred: Within a year I sent my stuff out to publishers. I entered contests. One of the biggest thrills of my writing life was when I won a short story contest sponsored by *The Capilano Review* literary magazine. It was the first real affirmation that I could write at a professional level. I have won many awards since, but none equalled the thrill of that first recognition.

After three or four years of writing short stories, and having them published by literary magazines, a collection of my stories was published by Oolichan Books. When the publisher first asked me to submit a manuscript to him (he had read some of my work) I laughed. I really thought he was kidding.

•

Mothers

They'll announce
I've had enough!
I'm letting go!

But when the child struggles
to loosen her hands
he finds himself in the grip
of two miniature pit bulls
Oh wait, she'll say

and when he runs to the gate
she'll follow, shameless –
you've forgotten your sweater
she'll call, your clean sox
why don't you stay
I'll cook you Kraft dinner

She was finished that woman
the day he staked out her womb

clung like a limpet
began padding his shadow bones
with her blood. She remembers
(mothers are always remembering)
when he was a baby –
how he screamed, eyes wild
the minute she left the room
Ah, she was his true love, his only

Now he wants
to go far away
He might phone, but
only for money
she'll try to hold him
the way she tried
(as a child) to hold the wild cat
they found in the barn

before it's over
(it'll never be over)
there'll be blood and howling.

Mildred Tremblay

10
Jenni Gehlbach

I first came across Jenni Gehlbach's writing when I saw a poem fastened to the wall in a community art show. I was intrigued and surprised by the addition of poetry to the art entries and also by the fact that I had known Jenni as a technical writer and had no idea she wrote poetry as well. (It was a good poem too!). Later she called me to ask advice about a poetry book that she was self-publishing.

Her background? Jenni Gehlbach was a technical writer and editor by profession. This included research reports, questionnaire design, business letters, technical and trades curriculum materials, procedural instructions. More recently Jenni has concentrated on editing (in some cases rewriting – ah! we know that kind of material only too well!). She comments on the connection between this kind of writing and poetry by saying "Clarity of language is the link, I think." Jenni turned to poetry in her 60s and self-published her first book of poetry, *Lines,* in 2005. Jenni, and her illustrator Tawny MacLachlan Capon, produced a very professional-looking book and gave themselves a fine launch party at their local marina.

She wished she hadn't left it so long before she started writing creatively and says that if she had started earlier, she would have had a better idea now of what works for others (readers that is) and what doesn't. Jenni doesn't accentuate the fact that time is more available in later years, since she had already used the time commuting to work by bus for her writing.

She does make a very interesting point, that for her, "Transitions both physical and emotional of various kinds appear to be motivational in my writing, though not necessarily in my themes." Yes, transitions throw one out of one's usual rut and into the unknown. This insecure place shakes one up, and often good writing comes out during these hungry ghost phases.

As to writing as an older person, Jenni wisely points out that one must be wary of "droning on and on about the past"; a definite negative that we all should look out for. We need to find how to use our past in a relevant manner for today's audience. "I think I am better able now," Jenni says, "than when I was young, to identify my reactions to life, rather than simply be awash in them. Also I have a longer experience from which to filter what I want to express. I have become a little less afraid of making a public ass of myself, which is enabling me to change my writing from being a very private act of self-expression to something that can be shared with others."

Here are Jenni's responses to the survey questions:

Naomi: *What made you start writing in your later years?*

Jenni: I suppose that in my earlier years, I simply didn't feel the urge to write creatively (as opposed to technically, connected with my work, of which I did a lot and with pleasure). I still don't have the urge to write imaginative prose. I distinctly remember saying in the summer of 1987 during a kayaking expedition "I wish I could write poetry," and Nick [her husband] saying, "Why don't you try?" So I did. In wishing to be able to write poetry, I wanted to express my thoughts combined with my feelings, I suppose, though I didn't analyze it at the time. Poetry seemed the right medium. I did not have a "story" to tell in short story, or novel form. I like the idea of concisely capturing a mood, or scene, or event (or all three together) in words.

Naomi: *How did you find your voice?*

Jenni: As to my voice, it just seemed to be in there, waiting to speak almost completed poems. A bit unnerving really. It's not something I have deliberately cultivated. One thing I would like to investigate is the extent to which I can control it.

Naomi: *In what form did you choose to express yourself?*

Jenni: Poetry offers the opportunity to express ideas and feelings succinctly and gracefully, without the need for imagined elaborate plots and characters as in even short stories. Also, by nature, it invites subtle wordplay, verbal echoes, associations, allusions, and alliteration (see!), and so on, which I love.

Naomi: *Did the process of writing change the way you think about yourself, and, if so, how?*

Jenni: Yes. I have never particularly thought of myself as having a creative imagination, having been told in art classes at school that I was bad at it. So it was a surprise and a great pleasure to find that I could do this at all, and a double pleasure to discover that some others like what I do.

Naomi: *What did you/are you doing with the material you have written?*

Jenni: I have self-published a collaborative book called *Lines* with an artist, Tawny MacLachlan Capon, which contains 48 poems, each with a related image. I also cheekily submitted one poem to a visual arts exhibit recently, gotta break down those rigid categories! And I am continuing to write poems. When I started writing poetry, I wasn't really considering publishing, merely expressing what I felt, saw, and thought. When I did think about publishing, I didn't imagine anyone "official" would want to publish my stuff. Also I felt my poems were often strongly visual and if I had had the talent would love to have been able to illustrate them myself. So I did the joint-project

I described above. I did the layout and design, a process I enjoy. The one great thing about self-publishing is the control one has over the look and physical feel of the book. The artist and I greatly enjoyed the process.

•

Christmas Rush

Christmas rush
Busily preparing,
dealing with the details of anticipated pleasure
almost
but not quite
drives out enjoyment of this moment.
My mind is busy with lists
as my hands roll and cut and fill and pinch,
my feet moving automatically from larder to counter to oven.
But I pause,
my nose filling with the sweet spice of mince pies,
and my ears are caught by the brilliance of trumpets
and the familiar joy of old carols
as dusk falls
and the house comes alive with lights.

Jenni Gehlbach

11 *Molly Ford*

I had always been interested in dance as a recreational activity and had studied ballroom dancing, folk dancing and flamenco. When I moved to my small island, I glanced over what was available, and found clogging lessons. It was at my clogging class that I met this amazing woman in her eighties...and could she clog!

Molly lives a life full of activity – clog dancing, involved in her church and in her community. Recently she completed an autobiography with her husband, Frank, for their children. Molly asked a friend to help her with the project. The friend arrived with a laptop and Molly and Frank told their stories, which the friend then transcribed. Sometimes Molly would write a story down in between her friend's visits. In that case, the friend would add the story to her files when she finished her visit. Molly is a lively talker and wanted to have that energy maintained in the final manuscript.

Molly is a good role model for non-writers who think they can't get it all down. Although she is a great letter writer, Molly had never tried anything more than getting a piece on her church's Strawberry Tea in the local paper. She knew she would need support if she was going to complete the project, so looked to a friend with writing skills for getting the material down on paper, and then chose a good local publisher to edit the manuscript, lay it out, and get it to a printer. She had the book done in both softcover and hardcover version. Because she was doing a short run (just for family members) this was a rather expensive venture.

Molly points out that one must be disciplined to be able to put extraneous matters out of mind and concentrate on one's chosen topic. "This is not always easy for the elderly," Molly continued, "for their powers of concentration tend to fade. For myself, having a rather chaotic mind, the discipline was both hard and cathartic, but always enjoyable."

Molly gives as pluses to being an older writer the fact that she, in spite of a wild social life, could set aside the time she needed to do the memoirs. She and her husband also have a rich life of experiences to look back on and to relate. She feels it's good for her and her husband's minds to delve back into the past and dredge up long-forgotten memories. "Solitary writing," Molly adds, "must be a much more difficult challenge, but with the two of us remembering, there was much laughter and even a few friendly arguments."

Here are Molly's responses to the survey:

Naomi: *What made you start writing in your later years?*

Molly: Our children were always asking us to record, either orally, or in print, some of the stories of our life. So now that we are in our 80s, we decided we had better get on with it.

Naomi: *How did you find your voice?*

Molly: I suppose my voice has always been there, hidden away. As a child I would write stories and in school I always enjoyed English composition classes. I am a terrible procrastinator when it comes to letter writing, but once started, the words flow. I am told by the recipients that they hear me talking in my letters – whether that is a good or bad thing is a moot point for I am quite long-winded.

Naomi: *In what form did you choose to express yourself?*

Molly: I would love to say I am a poet but I certainly am not. I find haiku fascinating since they produce such wonderful pictures in a few words – the opposite of my meanderings. I settled for writing the memoir because the children were constantly asking for it.

Naomi: *Did the process of writing change the way you think about yourself, and, if so, how?*

Molly: Not really except maybe to tell me I am not a [professional] writer.

Naomi: *What did you/are you doing with the material you have written?*

Molly: My husband and I have written our one book, *About Us* for a specific purpose. To tell our children and grandchildren the background of our parents' and our own lives, so different from anything they have experienced – living in India and Africa as children, boarding school days in England, early marriage years in Israel and finally emigrating to Canada where we started from scratch.

Molly and Frank launched *About Us* at Frank's 90th birthday party when their family and friends from church, clogging class, bridge club and discussion group could get together for a double celebration – book and birthday. Each child and grandchild received their own copy of the book, which took the entire print run.

•

From *About Us* by Molly and Frank Ford:

> My parents adopted me when I was a few months old. They then took the unusual step of not telling me of my adoption until I was twenty years old. Later in my life if, as a teacher, parents informed me that their child was adopted, I would say, "I hope he/she knows that he grew into your heart, not under it." My first reaction to my own news of adoption was of shock, followed closely by a second reaction "Whoopee! My dear cousin Frank is no longer my cousin!"
>
> Frank first heard of my adoption from his brother; apparently his reaction was "Hmmm, now I can look at her nice long legs!"
>
> So here we are sixty years later. Frank has lost much of his sight, but, he is still able to give me a gentle pat and say "Nice legs!"

12

Murray Barbour

I was very surprised when I was contacted by Murray about coming to our annual gathering of haiku writers on Gabriola Island, BC. Murray had been in the automotive and real estate business during his working life, and it was not until he was in his 90s that he turned to writing creatively. He remembered reciting poetry at high school and reading Shakespeare, but for his first writing attempts, Murray made the unusual choice of writing haiku. His images were strong and he did his best to pick up all the subtleties that go into writing what appears to be a very easy form of poetry, but which is one of the most difficult. He used simple everyday images that grabbed attention – the essence of haiku and the most likely way to enable the integrity of the writer's voice to come through.

Murray is a good example for those of you who think it is too late to begin. He began with the verve and enthusiasm of a much younger writer, and so can you. Since he was legally blind, he hired a secretary to write up his first poems, which he had himself written in large letters on the page. I remember seeing his first haiku written one per page. The large lettering and the great amount of white paper really added to those little poems from the void.

Here are Murray's responses to the survey questions:

Naomi: *What made you start writing in your later years?*

Murray: I'm legally blind, and so had time on my hands. I couldn't golf, drive or read and I couldn't stand TV.

Naomi: *How did you find your voice?*

Murray: I needed a hobby for therapeutic reason. I was inspired by Win Baker's [Winona Baker] success and by reading the haiku my wife, Florence's Grade 7 students wrote.

Naomi: *In what form did you choose to express yourself?*

Murray: For a while now, not knowing otherwise, I've used the traditional form of haiku i.e. 5-7-5 syllables, until I joined Haiku Canada Society in the fall of 2004 and found out I didn't need to be so strict with myself.

Naomi: *Did the process of writing change the way you think about yourself, and, if so, how?*

Murray: Changes, yes a few. I feel committed to produce poetry and enjoy every moment I spend using my brain that way.

Naomi: *What did you/are you doing with the material you have written?*

Murray: You [Naomi Beth Wakan] are the only person I have shared my material with. I just hope to keep on with writing haiku and other poetry and would like to send it to Haiku Canada competitions.

·

after the thunderstorm
loons plaintive cry
their nest afloat

hand in hand
matches father's steps
Mother's Day

how can I putt
double rainbow
over the bay

urn full of parsley
blue winter pansy
one interloper

early spring
swallows attack the old sofa
a soft nest

Murray Barbour

13 *Winona Baker*

When I first became interested in haiku, I scoured bookstores for books on the subject. I came across *Moss Hung Trees* and within it the excellent haiku that won Winona Baker a big prize ($1000) in Japan. Winona is one of the finest North American haiku writers and has been asked to judge many haiku competitions. She manages to hit the target almost every time with her haiku, and since Bashō claimed that he, himself, had only done 10 perfect haiku in his lifetime, that's saying a lot. Winona has won many awards including the most prestigious award in the haiku world – The Japanese Foreign Minister's Grand Prize presented during the International Section of the World Haiku Festival in Yamagata, Japan. Her books include: *Clouds Empty* (Red Cedar Press), *Not so Scarlet a Woman* (Red Cedar Press), *Moss Hung Trees* (Reflections), *Beyond the Lighthouse* (Oolichan Books), *Even a Stone Breathes* (Oolichan Books).

Winona's comments on the disadvantages of writing later in life are very perceptive. "Old age can shear off one's faculties. I used to pride myself on a good memory. It's humbling to have to write everything down. My flagging energy, I feel I could do more if I just didn't get tired. It takes effort to add, not just years to life, but life to years. Health problems such as a stiff neck and sore fingers after too long at the computer, as I forget to get up and stretch periodically, or go for a walk. One worries more about age-related illnesses, there are more doctor's visits consuming time. Also I don't handle stress as well as when I was young. Now doing one extra thing seems to take all day." Winona quotes Emily Dickinson: "Mine enemy is growing old."

She speaks of the problems of being part of a generation brought up without computers, feeling traumatized if her computer goes on the blink as she is so dependent on it and doesn't have a naturalness with it that young people do. Also as far as public readings of her poetry at night, Winona is less enthused, yet she recognizes that is just part of the writer's job and a way of saying thank you to the publisher.

Often older writers, such as Winona, are impatient with people who want you to make them into a writer, as Winona indicates, and she adds, as I also often want to say, "The free public library has books that can tell you more about writing than I can." It is not a lack of generosity, but recognition of the necessary hours that have to be put into the making of a writer.

As to the compensations of being an older writer, Winona points out that she can remember things from the time when she was very young, even if she can't remember everything about last week sometimes. She also endorses the general feeling of being less bothered by other's opinions. When asked to express a comment on someone else's poem in her writers' group, Winona is able to say, "It's your poem," and leave it at that.

About the psychological importance of writing, Winona shares a very common feeling that "Sometimes I feel I'm working on inner stuff that should have been solved in my youth. Still that could be grist for the mill." Ah! Don't we all feel that from time to time?

The loneliness and boredom sometimes seen in elderly people do not exist for Winona as she actually craves time to be alone for her writing. "I'm seldom bored," she says, "I always have something to do." Winona comments on writing filling the rest of her life, "Unless you lose your wits entirely, one should be able to work at writing until the end."

Winona Baker contributed this sensitive quote from Pat Lowther, "...it came to a choice/ whether to let her age-long labour fall/ grow old and bitter, turn her face to the wall/ or somehow to gather will..." Winona gathers will!

Here are Winona's responses to the survey questions:

Naomi: *What made you start writing in your later years?*

Winona: I'd always loved reading and enjoyed writing. I kept scribbler journals for years. I think I waited until my husband, four kids, aging parents, the PTA, the dog etc. were taken care of. I was shocked when I got breast cancer at 57. If I was ever going to quit saying I'll write some day it better be now I suddenly knew.

Naomi: *How did you find your voice?*

Winona: I'm not sure I have even now. Reading your words out loud helps. Where you hesitate, think 'this is not me.' Someone said that if you're a writer you don't concern yourself with what anyone else thinks or with pleasing anyone. My mother was quite moralistic so it took me a while to be able to follow my bliss as Campbell said. And who wants to hurt anyone?

Naomi: *In what form did you choose to express yourself?*

Winona: My mother knew hundreds of poems by heart, mostly by old dead white men, but it was good traditional poetry. No Walkmans clamped to our head then. We might be talking, singing or listening to mother reciting as we worked.

My father "kenned" the Gaelic, knew most of Burns by heart and sang his songs well, so poetry seemed a natural. I was writing rhyme at first. Then I took some creative courses at college to learn about the "moderns" such as Elliott, cummings and Pound.

Naomi: *Did the process of writing change the way you think about yourself, and, if so, how?*

Winona: After the Second World war women were expected to quit their jobs so the boys coming home could get work. You were expected to buy all the latest gadgets and fill your car with kids. If this depressed you, there was something the matter with you. I knew women who went around for years in Valium induced hazes. Poetry writing saved me.

Naomi: *What did you/are you doing with the material you have written?*

Winona: I submitted my work to publishers, but it's a time-consuming chore, even to journals and getting a book published seems to take longer the older you get. I self-published two books and they did okay, but I don't want to do it again because I am not a good sales person. Since then I have had several published by local publishers.

I do have stuff in drawers. If I'm lucky enough to keep my wits maybe more of it will appear in print. I should just shut my eyes and throw much in the recycle bag.

I've shared my writing with friends and family and have been praised for it especially when I write poems in remembrance of someone.

I've had lots of haiku published in literary magazines and anthologies, won many awards for

them, and had my poetry on Vancouver transit
buses.

•

moss-hung trees
a deer moves into
the hunter's silence

> *The above haiku won the Japanese Foreign*
> *Minister's Grand Prize, 1989*

my daughter cartwheels
between me and
the setting sun

it's happened
my mother doesn't know me –
first autumn rain

his size ten oxfords
on her dancing shoes –
even in the closet

family visit:
he tries to fix what's wrong
with the answering machine

on the shelter bench
waiting for the next bus
an empty pop can

> *Winona Baker*

14 Shirley Langer

Shirley Langer is a writer from Tofino. At one time in our quixotic life together, my husband and I bought a rural school house. We had noticed a very beautiful small inn on the way out from Toronto to our new property and it was there we decided to honeymoon. I remember knocking on the door and making my booking request only to be told that the small hotel had now become a private home and was no longer open. Shirley Langer was the woman who told me this news, a doctor's wife at that time, with a family of four lively teenagers.

So, I have known her family for a long time. They are all political, or environmental activists, and are against injustice everywhere. To this end, Shirley ran for mayor's office, to make local government more open and so became mayor of a small Ontario town for a while. This was an even greater involvement with the tangle of politics. It is not surprising then that some of her best writing has been articles for newspapers and magazines. She has, however, also won an award for a short story. After years of journalling, she has now turned to writing a young adult novel; her deep commitment to justice and social matters has led her to choose illiteracy as the book's theme. For those of you who are interested in writers' groups, Shirley has several supportive things to say about them.

On positive aspects about starting to write late in life, Shirley comments, "The advantage is the vantage point. Only the older person has a genuine vantage point to express, in any medium or activity, with ideas and perspectives about life and the living of it, gained by the experience of years and cumulative insight. A person who is not older can write about being old from the observer's vantage, and can do a good imitation. Only the older person can truly be it."

As to the negative aspects of writing later in life, Shirley regrets "The sedentary nature of the endeavour at a time in life when one should be physically active."

For those of you who would like to feel you are making a difference in the world with your writing – supporting a cause or defending a case – Shirley is a good role model for you.

Here are Shirley Langer's responses to the survey questions:

Naomi: *What made you start writing in your latter years?*

Shirley: I had been writing previously – poetry and journalling – but had never shared. Activism did motivate my writing with intention. In the late 1980s, when I was 50 plus, I was active in the field of community environmental advocacy. I did a lot of public speaking, some of which was extemporaneous, but most of which was prepared. The most consistent writing was a weekly article for the *Belleville Intelligencer,* Belleville, Ontario. In addition, a monthly article titled "It's Your Environment" was published in a regional magazine called *What's Happening?* After moving to Tofino in 1995, my writing diversified to include literary fiction, non-fiction and poetry.

Naomi: *How did you find your voice?*

Shirley: While I'm still trying to use my voice more honestly, rather than intellectually, the original challenge came from writer and activist, Betty Krawczyk, grandmother and published author, now 74. She said "Shirley, your writing is so interesting and accomplished, but we never learn a thing about what you are feeling; it's always so objective." I answered that I didn't know how to go about expressing my feelings; that committing my feelings to paper made me feel too self-conscious. Betty, undeterred, said (in her rich Mississippi accent) "Darlin' just start with the pronoun I, and don't let up." The very next work I undertook was a poem, which began with I. Betty's challenge opened the floodgates. I realized just how practical and locked up I had been in the creative process. I feel I lack the sensitivity and courage to speak honestly on the page; something I want to be able to do.

Naomi: *What form did you choose to express yourself in?*

Shirley: I didn't choose; as I mention above, I was challenged. While I continue to write prose, I'm attracted to poetry for its conciseness of form whereby the images and specific words serve as springboard, launching or tripping the reader into a bigger picture of emotions and ideas.

A word about setting up my writers' group, it wasn't difficult at all. Tofino being so small, 1200 people at that time, finding out who was writing, even who were closet writers was easy. The average regular participation every two weeks has been 6 – 12 people. Several of these people have produced published works over the years. Our aim, however, is to support one another in our quest to enhance our pleasure in writing, and to learn how to write effectively. The Clayquot Writers Group is still active today. New to the group are two scriptwriters, and an editor who wants to enter into creative writing.

Naomi: *Did the process of writing change the way you think about yourself?*

Shirley: Definitely. It began my opening up, and opened up more writing paths.

Naomi: *What did you/are you doing with the material you have written?*

Shirley: The writing group continues to meet regularly and support one another. There are workshops, readings, local publications. I am writing a book of historical fiction for young adults, and write a monthly article for a local magazine called *Tofino Times.* I am helping to organize a spoken word element in a local Arts event. In general, writing is a major part of my life.

•

From *Two Hundred Days that Changed Everything* by Shirley Langer

CHAPTER ONE

New Ideas
January 15, 1961

Anita sat alone in the velvety dark on the patio thinking about Conrado Benitez. Nobody in Cuba had known anything about Conrado a month ago. Now, everyone knew about the young volunteer teacher killed by counter-revolutionary rebels. So horrible! He had been on his way to teach his class – 44 children and a few adults – when he was captured by a band of counter-revolutionaries. They had staged a mock trial, found him guilty and condemned him to death by hanging for the crime of teaching literacy to peasants. His picture was everywhere. A dead teenage hero. Only seventeen. Her brother's

age. Anita shivered, though the tropical night air was still warm. People were writing poems and songs about him that appeared in the papers and on TV. A line from one she was learning at school came into her mind. "Whoever killed the present for you...did they believe they could kill the future?" Anita thought about Conrado's family. They must be so proud of him. He had been doing such a good thing, teaching illiterate people to read and write. But mostly, she knew they must be terribly sad.

15 Charles Roberts

I have never met Charles, but he was referred to me by one of his writers' group members as someone who would fit into my Late Bloomer theme, and e-mail acquaintance proved her right. Charles was a teacher, counsellor and administrator with a PhD in counselling psychology. Perfect background for a short story writer you might think, and you would be right, for Charles is a published short story writer. Seeing his stories in print has given him the confidence to see himself more as a professional writer. He has a supportive writer's group which he can't praise enough. To you writers out there who have a grievance that needs righting, Charles' method of fictionalizing past events may be just the example to follow when it comes to getting it off your chest. Also Charles found that by writing, his shadow side made an appearance. There is usually good material in these hidden aspects of ourselves that can be used for plots and themes, not to mention the therapeutic aspect of digging it up and out.

As a late writer Charles can chalk up a wealth of life experiences to write about. Also writing occupies his time now that he is less physically active. He complains that he has a lot to say and so little time to say it. True for many of us, I suspect.

His latest short story, "A Single Rose" appeared in the April/May/June issue of *The Storyteller*.

Here are Charles' responses to the survey questions:

Naomi: *What made you start writing in your later years?*

Charles: I had an unfortunate boss and when I eventually managed to leave my job, I wanted to write fiction telling about me and my boss; to get it off my chest as it were. I joined a writers' group to get some help with my writing. It soon became clear to me that something I had written in anger had few redeeming features. One member of the group was very helpful to me with all aspects of my writing.

Naomi: *How did you find your voice?*

Charles: I get an idea and sit down and write it out. Then I refine and refine and refine it. As you no doubt know, all writing is re-writing. At first I had difficulty with sitting back and looking objectively at what I had written. For this I found the opinion of those in the writing group I was in at the time to be invaluable, and now I feel I'm better at it. The "voice" that seems to best express what I want to say is writing in the first person.

Naomi: *In what form did you choose to express yourself?*

Charles: I have expressed myself mostly in short stories but do have two books completed after the first miserable try. I have only ventured into poetry a couple of times. I think short story writing is a good experience before turning to writing a novel. In a short story, what I have to say has to be said in a small amount of words. I'll always write short stories. In some ways short story writing takes more skill than writing novels.

Naomi: *Did the process of writing change the way you think about yourself, and, if so, how?*

Charles: Yes, indeed. Many of my short stories look at the dark side of life. The dark side is what seems to come out when I start a writing project. Realizing this has made me spend lots of time in self-exploration.

Naomi: *What did you/are you doing with the material you have written?*

Charles: I'm trying to get more short stories published. My reading tells me that a list of credits has some appeal to a prospective agent. I like sending off short stories but also would like, eventually, to have my books published.

•

From "Henry and Rachel", a short story Charles Roberts submitted to *The First Sentence*, a magazine that supplies the first sentence for writers to build on.

Having little to his name when he died, the reading of Henry Fromm's will went quickly. The only people present were Reverend Ballentine and the deacon of his church. I really didn't have to read the will to them because they, along with everybody else in town, already knew the few assets Henry had would go to the church. But Henry had wanted a formal reading, so I did it. I had been his lawyer for over thirty years. Henry died suddenly unlike Rachael, his wife. She lingered for several months, before breathing her last.

Their great disappointment was that they had been unable to produce children, but they always seemed happy even though we knew they were disappointed. Finally, after several years of miscarriages, there were no more pregnancies. Henry and Rachel seemed just the same. Maybe more relaxed. Everyone was relieved. All that happened about fifty years ago, but those of us still alive remember. Nobody's business is private in this town.

16 Maralee Gerke

Maralee and her husband Robin were vacationing on Gabriola when I met them at my husband's favorite swimming spot. Gabriolans are friendly folk, and as these people came from away (actually far away in Oregon), we were soon filling them in with information on the island's features. Maralee had been a teacher for 21 years. She taught all grades from kindergarten to high school. She also had worked five years as a school librarian.

Maralee is a self-published poet (*Looking Back, Facing Forward* – a chapbook) writing in a small town, and very much enjoying the support of her writers' group there. She is producing her latest self-published book, *Like Pearls on My Tongue,* with her husband, the photographer Robin Gerke. It is a very professional-looking book, perfect bound, with a great cover outside (and fine poems inside). If you have decided to self-publish, it is a wonderful help if a member of the family can assist your book's layout and cover.

Maralee Gerke considers the best thing about writing later in life to be having the time to write. She doesn't feel there really is a downside to being an older writer because so long as she is creating she feels truly alive and young inside. When pressed, she says that, "The worst thing is not taking advantage of the time I have available to write. Also I have found that my recall of vocabulary isn't as good as it used to be, so I keep a thesaurus handy. Another hard thing is not being around young writers enough. They have a vitality that I think would be good for older writers to be around."

Here are Maralee's responses to the survey questions:

Naomi: *What made you start writing in your later years?*

Maralee: There were several reasons that I started writing seriously at age 55. First I was retiring from a long career in teaching and wanted to have something that would keep me mentally alert and in touch with the world. I also faced a cancer diagnosis and came to the realization that life is not infinite and if I wanted to write, I should not hesitate. The final reason I became a writer was that no one in my family was a writer and I wanted to leave some written record for my sons. I wanted them to know a little about their mother and her interior life.

Naomi: *How did you find your voice?*

Maralee: I think I haven't found it entirely yet, but the best way for me is to write and rewrite until the poem says what I want it to say. I keep reading books of other poets and fiction. I write down words or phrases that have the music of language in them.

I keep a journal of these. I reread them from time to time for inspiration, and then go back to work. Writing is the hardest work I have ever loved.

Naomi: *In what form did you choose to express yourself?*

Maralee: I write poetry. I have written some rhyming poetry, but mostly free or blank verse. I am doing more exploring of form since I attended a poetry workshop this summer.

Naomi: *Did the process of writing change the way you think about yourself, and, if so, how?*

Maralee: I think that writing has given me the sense that I do have an intellect and I can use it every day. It has also made me know that every person's story is important. Being part of a writers' group has helped me bring my writing out into the air. I have more confidence in my voice. I have done a poetry reading and it has helped me to have more presence in a group.

Naomi: *What did you/are you doing with the material you have written?*

Maralee: I have sent in many poems and had quite a few published in poetry journals. I have also self-published a chapbook of poetry and am working on a new one. I have won several contests and placed in several others. I have spoken to women's groups and read poems for them.

•

Sidewalk Revelation

A footprint
Near a new fire hydrant
On the sidewalk.
The brave testament of a passerby
Leaving his impression on the world.

The wet cement an invitation to immortality.
A quick glance around
The street fortuitously empty
The tennis-shoed foot pressed down firmly.
Complete the print distinct and final.

That print stared up at me.
"I'm here to stay," it seemed to say.
I wished that it were my foot emblazoned there.
That anonymous step attaining,
What I strive for.

Maralee Gerke

17 Adrienne Kemble

One meets Late Bloomers in all kinds of places, and I met Adrienne Kemble when looking at her house for possible purchase. Like many people of her era, she had married early and had children. In her 30s she found herself divorced and on her own with four children. Adrienne went back to school and finished her Anthropology degree and continued on to a MA in Sociology. She worked as a counsellor at a community college for 20 years and, after a second divorce, realized she needed to do something very different, so she took six months leave and went to West Africa.

After an early retirement Adrienne joined CESO, where she has worked as a volunteer advisor on projects in aboriginal communities here in Canada as well as on projects overseas: in Guyana, Guatemala, Kyrgyzstan and Bolivia. During this time Adrienne was also a purchaser for Global Village, a fair-trade, non-profit organization. On this she comments, "This work coincided nicely with my CESO activities, and I was able to work closely with artisans (mostly women), desperately trying to feed their families." From this rich life and wide travels, Adrienne has started writing some very interesting pieces – not exactly travelogues, since they move inside much more than outside.

Adrienne feels that, as a Late Bloomer, she gets an opportunity to see her life in perspective, even if she's writing about something quite removed from herself. As she puts it so well, "I'm still in the background thinking." She also points out that writing is a great occupation for days that might be too long, especially for people who live alone as she does.

Adrienne says the thing she likes best about writing in her dotage [her word] is that she knows she CAN write, so she doesn't have to spend a lot of time questioning her ability, and that leaves her free to just write. She doesn't really care what other people think of her writing and doesn't want to be part of a writing group critiquing each others' work unless they are very much better than her.

Many of the writers I spoke to wish they hadn't left it so long before beginning to write. Adrienne asks, "Why did I leave it so late in taking myself seriously as a writer?" She feels it's almost too late to start flogging her work and learning the skills to do that, which are, as she points out, quite different from the skills required to be a writer.

Here are Adrienne's responses to the survey questions:

Naomi: *What made you start writing in your later years?*

Adrienne: I had always written bits and pieces here and there, usually when I was in crisis, and always tore them up and threw them away. There is already a writer in my family and so I wasn't encouraged to take myself seriously. I have always used writing as a form of therapy, but have been writing regularly probably for the past ten years. I had always used writing as a means of keeping my thoughts straight and, of course, kept copious diaries of my overseas adventures, which I have rewritten on returning home.

Naomi: *How did you find your voice?*

Adrienne: I am flattered that you assume I have a voice. I just sit down and "me" pours out...

Naomi: *In what form did you choose to express yourself?*

Adrienne: Short expository pieces, never fiction. I don't think I have a good enough imagination to write fiction, and anyway have been kept quite busy just remembering and writing about my own adventures.

Naomi: *Did the process of writing change the way you think about yourself, and, if so, how?*

Adrienne: Writing hasn't really changed the way I think about myself, but it certainly helps/forces me to organize my thoughts, and gives me some sort of discipline in my thinking that I have trouble achieving in speaking... I seem to be able to be much more fluent in my writing. I have never experienced writer's block, but probably because I only write when I want to, not when I have to.

Naomi: *What did you/are you doing with the material you have written?*

Adrienne: Nothing much so far – I did send one piece off to the BBC International Writer's Competition (nothing like starting big!) I haven't heard the results yet, but am certainly not holding my breath.

•

I wrote this about my time in West Africa, when I was invited to attend the funeral of the aged wife of a long-dead paramount chief.

– Adrienne Kemble

Members of the Women's Society were in charge of the event. After a few minutes one of the women approached me and asked in a conversational tone "Would you like to view the corpse?" My immediate reaction was to decline, but conscious of my good manners, I agreed and was led into the house. There in the parlour, lying on a trestle table amid flickering candles, lay the corpse, an incredibly aged soul, wrinkled and shrivelled, a scrap of what had once been a

woman, wrapped in traditional dyed garah cloth.
Circling the corpse, chanting funereal dirges, was
a long line of women. No men. A space was made
for me, and I joined the group. Occasionally as
she passed, a woman would stop, lean over and
kiss the cheek of the corpse. I assumed they held
a special relationship to her, but as I approached,
the line-up stopped, and my sponsor in loud
solemn tones announced "You may kiss the
corpse." I felt that everyone's eyes were on me.
What had caused her demise? A myriad of
hideous tropical diseases flashed through my
mind. Strangely, old age did not occur to me. I
knew I had to do it. I leaned over and touched
her soft, cool cheek with my lips. At that moment
I felt a fleeting kinship with this woman. Where
had her life taken her? Probably to some of the
places I too had been – wife, mother – and here
we were sharing a moment together, she in
death, I in life.

18
Jim Swift

Jim was born in the UK, and was educated at Chislehurst and Cambridge. He taught in Kenya, in Ontario and in British Columbia before retiring to Port Alberni with his wife, Judy. Here is a writer who started writing only after retiring from a long career as a Math professor and Computer Coordinator. He combines his writing with another love, photography, to produce stunning haiga (haiku with accompanying illustrations). Jim's haiga have recently been displayed at several BC Galleries. I first met Jim when he approached me, in my role of poetry-editor, for input for his first chapbook of poems. I saw a certain sensitivity in his work and was delighted to encourage him.

Jim, because he is starting to write late in life, regrets that he might not have time to complete what he is trying to do. He adds that, "By starting something later in life, it means that you are probably not able to amass 30 – 40 years of experience, or mastery. The experience will therefore have more of the characteristics of a beginner, but age can give you the wisdom to savour the state of a beginner." A useful attitude to have.

Here are Jim's responses to the survey questions:

Naomi: *What made you start writing in your later years?*

Jim: When I was living at Chapel Hill, I went to the Society of Friends meetings. One or two people were looking for a ride to a conference led by the poet, David Whyte. It sounded interesting, so I offered to drive.

The conference was not about poetry, per se, but David used poetry to make his points in the plenary sessions. Between the sessions there were various working groups and I joined one called "writers of the mind." I had never thought of myself as a writer, nor read much poetry, but that group seemed the most interesting of the available study groups. I decided that I would use the opportunity to write my first poem. I spent two days in that group, but by the end of the two days I had written a poem and just went from there.

Naomi: *How did you find your voice?*

Jim: I wrote about the things that I found interesting. After I retired, I returned to an old love – photography – and started to put poetry to photographs. Later, after attending an inspiring meeting of the Haiku BC (now pacifi-kana) group, I found much similarity between photography and haiku and since then my writing has been in that form. Both photography and haiku are about "being in the moment." I don't care to analyze such things though.

Naomi: *In what form did you choose to express yourself?*

Jim: Short verse originally, now haiku

Naomi: *Did the process of writing change the way you think about yourself, and, if so, how?*

Jim: This is a difficult question to answer. I suppose, like most people, I find it all too easy to get caught up in the past or the future. For some time I have wanted to develop the ability to see at a more focused level than I have been used to.

Jay Maisel, a great photographer said that, "Being a good photographer means you have to have the ability to extract a passionate amount of joy from things other people find commonplace or overlook completely." I think that this also applies to the art of haiku.

So, in the sense that hoping that being in these fields will allow me to develop the ability to see, then yes, maybe the process of writing is changing the way that I think about myself and the way that I think.

Naomi: *What did you/are you doing with the material you have written?*

Jim: Sharing it with haiku and haiga groups on the Internet. I have not yet submitted it to publishers or self-published. I also share my work with friends and family.

Jim's photographic haiga and haiku have now appeared on many e-zines and in group shows. Some of Jim Swift's favorite haiga websites are:

Simply Haiku www.simplyhaiku.com

Haiku Hut www.haikuhut.com

Haiga Online www.haigaonline.com

Ron Moss www.ronmoss.com

•

**the ocean plays
to an audience of one
drawn to listen
he also hears
the waves within**

**surrounded by mountains
I try to photograph
the icy wind**
(World Haiku Review)

**breakfast couple
the sentences of her hands
punctuated by his feet**
(Hermitage 2005)

Late Bloomer: On Writing Later in Life

grey day
a cloud-break paints
the sun across Skye

(Simply Haiku)

Jim Swift

19 Leanne McIntosh

Leanne was born and raised in Regina, Saskatchewan. As a small child writing took on a special meaning for Leanne since, with her father away at war, letters and pictures were the only way she knew her father. His letters were read aloud to her and a drawing or printing by her was always included in the return post. So writing was special for her from an early age. Later in her life, Leanne like Mildred Tremblay, started with short stories and then switched to poetry.

I first met her when she read at a poetry festival I was organizing. I was impressed by her quiet but strong presence and have been impressed ever since as I become more and more familiar with her poetry.

Leanne makes the interesting comment that she was an excessively private person, as many of our jottings and diaries make us, and so she started to share herself and her wonderful poetry: *The Sound the Sun Makes* (Oolichan Books), *The Attitude of the Tree: Sixteen Tao poems* (Leaf Press), *Liminal Space* (Oolichan Books). By putting her writing out Leanne fulfils two purposes – to share her being and to share her talent.

When asked about the positives of being a Late Bloomer, Leanne McIntosh puts it well, "One quality I bring to my late-in-life writing career is confidence...confidence to speak boldly but also to be tender and vulnerable. I have little to lose – too old to be famous and rejection is familiar enough to have lost its power. Writing has become a way of living a solitary life in the world as it is both voice and silence."

Here are Leanne's responses to the survey questions:

Naomi: *What made you start writing in your later years?*

Leanne: I'd say I was impelled over a lifetime. Reading and writing were sources of consolation and revelation within a world I shared with no one. One day it dawned on me I was excessively private and people knew me only by a series of roles. I realized if I wanted to be seen and known, welcomed and valued, then I needed to open my inner world to others. Writing was a familiar tool.

Naomi: *How did you find your voice?*

Leanne: I think voice is not so much a style of writing as an articulation of a way of being. Voice isn't found, but it's always evolving. Voice is inherent and blooms, periodically, in passion. Voice is the silence in the poem. Voice is the gold coin on an open palm.

Coming as I do from Saskatchewan, my voice is wheat fields and sunsets; it's a Gregorian chant and Catholic theology. My voice is the rough edge of a high school education and the work place. It's arms to hold a husband, five children and my twelve grandchildren. My voice was strong during my husband's dying and death and now, in widowhood, it's young again, retracing the steps, remembering who I was at 22 when I married and changed my name.

Naomi: *In what form did you choose to express yourself?*

Leanne: I'd lived in Nanaimo for about 20 years, my children grown up, when I began taking writing courses at the local college. I helped my husband occasionally at his real estate office, but had time enough for my own pursuits. I chose the writing course because I had knowledge of the instructor and that course set me onto short stories. When in 1991 my husband was diagnosed with cancer, I found poetry had the ability to quickly move to the emotional heart of the situation and my love affair with poetry began in earnest. I think, too, poetry has the personal revelation I appreciated in my childhood experience of letter writing.

Naomi: *Did the process of writing change the way you think about yourself, and, if so, how?*

Leanne: I think the process of writing changed other people's perception and estimation of me. So, in a circular way, I grew more confident and experienced a higher level of satisfaction with my life, which encouraged me to write more.

Writing has become my practice, my path, poetry the scripture. I read the work of other poets for inspiration and encouragement. I think I've been humanized through the process of writing, more willing to be vulnerable. And, I've grown bolder, my voice stronger. Writing is teaching me to live with paradox.

Naomi: *What did you/are you doing with the material you have written?*

Leanne: Some I submitted to publishers and others I put it in a drawer. Oolichan Books published my latest manuscript, *Liminal Space,* in Fall 2005. Since *Liminal Space,* I've written more poems, submitted to literary journals, rewritten, submitted again. A fresh spiral on the way to another manuscript.

•

Ground Hog Day

The sharpness of my shadow startles me. I set aside the shears
and return to my familiar kitchen, to a cup of coffee
and my favorite Spanish monks chanting the Kyrie.
I play the music louder than a teenager, louder
than the pipe organ rattled the stained-glass windows
in the convent chapel where Mother Theodore sat
in the front pew, her hands hidden under her scapular
while a priest from Muenster listed the evils of country dances.
I lived in the city and without a car or someone to take me,
I missed the reason a girl needs the Virgin Mary to dance
between her and a swaying boy. I went to confession anyway.
That's how my life's been, more fear than grace. I've never
taken a chance on my darkest parts, the woman without a voice
locked away like a family secret. Poems open the door.
I rummage for a phrase to take me beyond
a rope two feet shorter than the length of a man
into a fairy tale. A Marilyn Monroe descent into sleep
with an empty pill bottle and an open phone line,
the late-night radio host explaining his theory of hollow planets.
Imagine the earth with no fiery core, its body crumpled into a fist.
Or the silky slit of a razor in a warm bath. Death
seen through the wine bottle's green glass. In the first of my poems
I was too shy to lift the skirts of desire. But this afternoon
accompanied by singing monks and thirty poems
I finger the thorn of a rose.

Leanne McIntosh

20
John Nesling

I want to accentuate that not all folks who start writing late in life will achieve, or even want to reach, fame and fortune. Many want the very real and important record of the past to be set down for their children and grandchildren. I have known John Nesling and his family for more than 30 years and have watched John, and his wife, Lilian, build a home on one remote BC island and build a boat on another. While John had kept diaries, his writing had mainly been restricted to letters to his family and to the editors of local newspapers. However, here is a writer who eventually "got it all down" in his 70s as a record for his large family. John, who had pioneering experience in New Zealand, Australia and Canada, managed to finish *The Long Way Round* – an account of his years in the Australia outback which he is self-publishing.

When it comes to autobiography and memoir writing, John Nesling points out how painful it can be for an older person, "It forces you to relive the past – often with regret about all the things you didn't get right." He asks, "Why ever didn't one realize how good life was at the time instead of only now – in retrospect?" John does find a brighter side to his question saying, "There is a notion that perhaps it had to be that way so that looking at one's life backwards may help to make sense of it, since one is forced to reflect." However, he also quotes Mordecai Richler as a warning. Richler referred to autobiography as an enormous conceit [intended] to impose meaning on being here.

Here are John's responses to the survey questions:

Naomi: *What made you start writing in your later years?*

John: If you keep a rough diary you may be able to write something of a biographical nature and at least get the chronology right. Then if you write something when you are still quite young and read it ten years later, you may be unhappy with it; if you read it 20 years later you may be glad you didn't publish it. Now 30 years later the drivel you have written may really embarrass you. You'll need to tear it up. You may discover that it was a shocking indulgence full of yourself and your own awful youthful ego. Finally you will get closer to the bone and struggle to leave yourself and your ego out of it as much as possible. A paradox, but never mind – you tried. After another 10 years, if it looks almost OK, you may be inclined to clean it up and publish it. Hence "a slow and ponderous process." And, of course, if being a writer is not your regular business, then it may well have taken this long – albeit with the idea always at the back of your mind. The propensity was always there, after all.

Naomi: *How did you find your voice?*

John: As I've just written, by having lots to say about things and a propensity for writing them down on paper – a slow, ponderous process with a better chance of coming out right.

Naomi: *In what form did you choose to express yourself?*

John: Prose.

Naomi: *Did the process of writing change the way you think about yourself, and, if so, how?*

John: Somewhat. Made me realize my intellectual limitations and lack of suitable academic background. You should tread carefully around those things for which you don't have a suitable academic background obviously – lest your writing become phoney. So depending on what you want to write, lack of suitable background can be an impediment. In the end you're limited to writing about what you know. It seems important to be hard on yourself – accept your limitations.

Naomi: *What did you/are you doing with the material you have written?*

John: Self-publishing. The family are well aware of this book and many of them have contributed in one way or another – it pleases them and they are looking forward to reading it, and so am I. My son is formatting it. This being a biographical episode, it probably will enhance the family's understanding of things.

•

From *The Long Way Round*, by John Nesling:

Thus it was one fine Saturday morning, shopping in Flinders Street that such thoughts were given vent. Standing outside a chemist shop while Lilian is making hasty purchases inside for her pending confinement, I am approached by a large non-uniformed, but obvious policeman. He may even have revealed his identity, though Lilian swears he wore a uniform, but the assured air of authority would have been enough. "Why don't you shave?" With mouth open in startled amazement at this obvious rebuke, I may have stuttered – "What—?" Beards were uncommon at that time, but surely not worthy of police interest. Perhaps I uttered something; he may already have done a metaphorical 'oops' by the time Lilian emerged in all her radiant, pregnant splendour. She took in the whole situation – got it in one – seeming to go up him one side and down the other – exploding – giving vent to all the pent up emotion and frustration arising from her vastly changed situation. And here was a tangible enemy – someone who epitomized the whole problem – standing now on one leg, now on the other – taking the brunt of her raving. Bumbling, stumbling, attempting explanation – onlookers becoming entertained. Looking the other way in case she turned her fury on me, I told her "for God's sake

shut up," so the poor fellow could slink away. Tangling with a woman, especially a pregnant woman, was definitely not on his agenda. Not long afterwards Lilian quit work and Christmas in the opposite season was endured.

Historically well-founded dislike of authority is deeply entrenched into the Australian psyche – and resentment of police in North Queensland seemed not entirely without cause. Stories of police antics and their ill-treatment of people were so numerous that one might wonder whether their function was to protect or harass the public. So a beard in this somewhat frontier town of the 50s was cause for suspicion? Australia's "Mainstreet" perhaps – a comparison to be made with American small mid-western towns of previous decades. But these thoughts and weeping and gnashing of teeth were soon eclipsed by an entirely new life. Our novel situation spared us so much of the pain suffered by many of those emigrants who remained in the larger cities. We were exploring.

21 *Roy Innes*

I like to go to book launches; all writers need encouragement and I do my bit. I met Roy at his book launch, and, buying the book he was promoting, I was delighted to find it captivating, and very accomplished for a first detective story. Roy is a doctor who started writing on retirement with this whiz-bang detective story, *Murder in the Monashees,* which is a winner. He has a wonderful background for such writing, being a retired doctor and outdoorsman. He tells of going on hikes with his brother in the wilds of Saskatchewan at twenty below. "We'd light a fire to cook a can of Campbell's soup (still one of my most memorable gourmet meals) and sink gently into six foot snow-drifts." Later Roy worked outdoors to pay his way through medical school – as a logger, forest-research worker, farm hand, surveyor's assistant – all good grist for the writing mill. Roy has done his share of climbing, "I always enjoyed the struggle to the top and the view when I got there," he says, as well as fishing, canoeing, camping and cycling. Hunting is still one of his favourite outdoors activities.

Roy is a lesson to all you Late Bloomers to look at your life-skills and see if they direct you into a particular form of writing as they did with him.

Roy points out that "Laziness, objection to deadlines, the tedium of editing, a fear of marketing – are all common with age and retirement. I think this is particularly true of men who place not having to go to work everyday on a par with being let out of school for the summer holidays. Most authors, I think, focus best when starving and having to make a living writing." With the latter statement, I heartily agree.

Roy adds that, "When older, writing skills are rusty, especially if work demanded none. Secretaries were doing it all for you – spelling, grammar, composition and especially typing – skills are dormant for too long." He adds that it is the same for computer savvy.

Roy Innes makes the interesting point that since one has possibly read so many books, there is a tendency to mimic good writers. This is particularly true when the older writer is struggling to be different, to find a unique plot and characters and his or her voice. Another way of losing one's voice, according to Roy, is to take too many courses, writing to the dictates, styles and tastes of the instructors. A third way is to seek too much advice. "Even editors," Roy points out, "can make so many changes that your voice disappears completely."

Like others, Roy finds retention of brilliant ideas is inversely proportional to age and actually carries an old hand-held Dictaphone to use when he is exercising and doesn't have pen, paper or sticky notes handy. As he complains, "In my youth I had a photographic memory. Now there doesn't appear to be room for any more than a thought at a time and it's erased quickly when a new one arrives. Of course, the ideas themselves come more slowly with age but they do come and there's time to mull thoughts over rather than blurting them down on paper to meet a deadline."

Roy went on a tour to launch his book...not quite as exciting as some of you may think. As he wittily says, "My sense of dignity is too high. To sit at a card table in a mall in front of a bookstore hoping that a passerby will be interested enough to stop and chat and maybe even buy a book is not something that I am comfortable with. The travel, the late nights, the endless cups of coffee, wine and cheese, lack of exercise and general disruption of my routine takes a toll. It takes me days to recover from one of these [book-promoting tours]. Often the audience (of maybe six) write themselves (or think they probably could) and are more interested in how to manage to get published than in appreciating your work."

"It's amazing," Roy says, "That publicity people assume writers are automatically good public readers and comfortable on stage or before cameras. Some are, I'm sure, but most of us are comfortable only in front of our computer screens. Public anything is scary."

Of the launch Roy did on his home ground, (the launch where I met him), Roy comments, "A number of people knew me on the island as one of the morning regulars at Suzy's restaurant, as a golfer, a hunter. It came as quite a shock to most that I actually was a writer. That brought out the expected reaction – if I could do it so could they – hence a lot of questions about publishing. Seriously though, I felt a warmth and genuine congratulatory aura at that launch – recognition from friends, neighbours and fellow writers. What better reward, eh?"

Here are Roy's responses to the survey questions:

Naomi: *What made you start writing in your later years?*

Roy: The obvious answer is that I now have the time – the precious commodity appreciated most, I think, when the years of obligatory schooling, work and support of children are behind one. Doctors and golf go together for some reason. Even in our mild climate (on the west coast), however, golf is not a 365 day a year activity. It rains a lot and occasionally snows. I had to find something else to occupy my time and writing fit the bill.

          In truth, though, the reason for my writing goes deeper than that. Creativity, I think, is a basic urge in everyone and most try to fulfill it. Whether it's oil painting, making music, potting, restoring old cars, or growing things, it doesn't matter. One needs a creative outlet. Writing has been mine – newsletters, letters to friends, etc. Even in my academic life, some of my departmental budget proposals, I'm embarrassed to say, contained an element of creative fiction.

Typing "The End", printing out the manuscript, looking at it neatly stacked on your desk and receiving word from the publisher that you've done something the world wants to read – I can't imagine the artist, the architect, the playwright or the composer feeling any more satisfied. That's why I write.

Naomi: *How did you find your voice?*

Roy: I enjoy the role of storyteller. It's an art, either in oral form or by use of the written word. Unless one is mimicking the style of others, everyone's voice is unique and comes out in the telling. Finding your voice, in my opinion, occurs simply by using it. Written or in speech, it comes out on its own. It may not be attractive to others, in which case obscurity is the result, but enjoyment can still be had. On a personal basis, being able to play a musical instrument, sing, paint, sculpt, or write is an accomplishment in itself. The pleasure in being artistically creative goes back to the lone caveman scratching images on a rock.

Naomi: *In what form did you choose to express yourself?*

Roy: I tend to be a daydreamer and so writing fiction comes more easily to me. Non-fiction is more akin to the research and scientific papers I was required to produce in my working years. I've had enough of that kind of realism. "Fun" is the operative word with my life now and fiction writing fits nicely into that philosophy.

Naomi: *Did the process of writing change the way you think about yourself, and, if so, how?*

Roy: Only when my first novel was accepted for publication. The realization that I could write something that was commercially acceptable came as a pleasant surprise. My ego swelled accordingly until I realized how big and deep the mystery of the writing pond was. As I work on a second novel, humility has returned.

Naomi: *What did you/are you doing with the material you have written?*

Roy: Most of what I've written sits deep in the bowels of my computer. My first novel and the Gabriola Rod and Gun Club Newsletter are my only exposures to the public at the moment.

•

From *Murder in the Monashees,* by Roy Innes.

The Monashee Mountains in southern British Columbia are more foothills of the Rockies than true mountains in a picture-book sense. They don't have sharp, snow-capped peaks, but are spectacular in their own way. The late fall is particularly beautiful when the needles of the larch trees turn a brilliant yellow. Typically they grow in bunches amongst the pines, spruce and fir, creating a canvas of dark shades of green splashed with gold. Many second and third growth plots within the older unharvested stands give a variation in texture. The creeks, running deep then shallow and falling into gorges, add blues and whites to the palette as well as sound and motion to break the stillness of the forest. A photographer gazing upon all of this would be annoyed, however, by two jarring, man-made blemishes. First, ugly brown scars of logging roads cut into the greenery as they snaked their way to the peaks and second, just below one ridge, a dot of fluorescent orange glowed unnaturally. Zooming in, the camera would reveal this dot to be a toque warming the head of a hunter lying prone in the snow. Russell Montgomery was mumbling to himself as he peered through his rifle's scope at a thicket 75 yards ahead of him. Behind it, he knew, was a large mule deer stag.

22

A final word

Now I have presented you with 14 people who have started to write late in their lives. None of us has garnered fortunes and only two or three of us have gathered a small amount of fame, yet all of us have achieved something in our writing – a closure to the past, a healing in the present, a promise for the future. We are not an exclusive group. We invite you to join us. Please do.

My small square

My life is like a small square
that I choose to live within.
Outside is no more evil
than inside, for, being
human, all qualities, good,
or bad, are to be found in
this skin/flesh/bone bag of nonsense,
albeit drawn modest.
Inside my boundaries,
I write of spiders scattering
from a clothes-pin bag and
the unsuspected autumn crocus
purpling the ground –
petty things, yet, within
my small square, they
fill to the corners.

Naomi Beth Wakan

23 *Web resources*

Websites and grants of interest to older writers – please remember, as I mentioned before, that these come into being and pass away faster than restaurants:

www.kimberlyripley.writergazette.com
(Contains interesting articles.)

www.speculativeliterature.org
(Older writers grant for fantasy, horror, folk tales etc.)

www.pw.org/frequently_asked_questions/qcms.php
(A poets and writers site.)

www.theroseandthethornezine.com/Newsletter/August2 003.htm#Article
(Am I too Old to Start Writing?)

www.underdown.org/mf-late_blooming.htm
(Late Blooming Writers can succeed.)

creativewriting.gmu.edu/faculty/personal/cheuse
(An article on starting late, by Alan Cheuse.)

www.kezimatthews.com/late_bloomers.htm
(An article on Late Bloomers. Enter www.kezimatthews.com and highlight Late Bloomers.)

www.societyofauthors.net
(The Sagittarius Prize, for a first novel by an author over 60.)

24 *Bibliography*

Baker, Winona. *Not so Scarlet a Woman.* Nanaimo: Red Cedar Press, 1987.

Baker, Winona. *Clouds Empty Themselves: Island Haiku.* Nanaimo: Red Cedar Press, 1998.

Baker, Winona. *Moss-Hung Trees: Haiku of the West Coast.* Gabriola Island: Reflections Publishing, 1992.

Baker, Winona. *Beyond the Lighthouse.* Lantzville: Oolichan Books, 1992.

Baker, Winona. *Even a Stone Breathes.* Lantzville: Oolichan Books, 2000.

Bolker, Joan. *The Writer's Home Companion.* New York: Henry Holt, 1997.

Byers, Stephen. *Creative Writing for Senior.,* ebook ed., Self-published, 2005.

Canton, Alan N. *The Silver Pen: A Writing Guide for Seniors.* California: Adams-Blake Publishing, 1996.

Coberly, Lenore M. *Writers Have No Age.* New York: Haworth Press, 2005.

Cool, Lisa Collier. *How to Write Irresistible Query letters.* Cincinnati: Writer's Digest Books, 1990.

Deutsch, Babette. *Poetry Handbook.* New York: HarperCollins, 1982.

Ford, Molly and Frank. *About Us.* Self-published, 2005.

Gehlbach, Jenni. *Lines,* Self-published, 2005.

Gerke, Maralee. *Looking Back, Facing Forward.* chapbook, Self-published, 2006

Gerke, Maralee , illus. Robin Gerke. *Like Pearls on My Tongue,* self-published, 2005

Innes, Roy. *Murder in the Monashees.* Edmonton: NeWest Publishers Ltd, 2005.

Jackman, Ian. *The Writer's Mentor.* New York: Random House, 2004.

Kazemek, Francis. *Exploring our Lives.* Santa Monica: Santa Monica Press, 2002.

Levin, Donna. *Get that Novel Started.* Cincinnati: Writer's Digest Books, 1992.

Levin, Donna. *Get that Novel Written.* Cincinnati: Writer's Digest Books, 1996.

Lyon, Elizabeth. *A Writer's Guide to Fiction.* New York: Perigree Books, 2004.

McIntosh, Leanne. *The Sound the Sun Makes.* Lantzville: Oolichan Books, 2003.

McIntosh, Leanne. *The Attitude of the Tree: Sixteen Tao poems.* Lantzville: Leaf Press, 2003.

McIntosh, Leanne. *Liminal Space.* Lantzville: Oolichan Books, 2005.

Nesling, John. *The Long Way Round,* Self-published,

Nye, Naomi Shihab, *The Same Sky,* Aladdin, 1996.

Oliver, Mary. *A Poetry Handbook.* New York: Harcourt, 1995.

Ripley, Kimberly. *Free Lancing Late in Life.* Booklocker.com, 2001.

Thair, Maree. *Highlights of our Lives.* British Columbia: College of New Caledonia, 1998.

See, Carolyn. *Making a Literary Life.* New York: Random House, 2002.

Strand, Mark, *Reasons for Moving,* New York: Scribner, 1972.

Terayama, Katsujō and Ōmori Sogen, *Zen and the art of Calligraphy: The essence of sho,* translation John Stevens, London: Routledge and Kegan Paul Books Ltd., 1983.

Tremblay, Mildred. *Dark Forms Gliding.* Lantzville: Oolichan Books, 1988.

Tremblay, Mildred. *Old Woman Comes Out of her Cave.* Lantzville: Oolichan Books, 2001.

Tremblay, Mildred. *The Thing About Dying.* Lantzville: Oolichan Books, 2005.

Turco, Lewis. *The Book of Forms.* University Press of New England, 1986

Wakan, Naomi Beth. *Memory Bag.* Qualicum Beach: Lightsmith Publishing, 1999.

Whitman, Ruth. *Becoming a Poet.* self-published, 1982.

Whitworth, John. *Writing Poetry.* St. Neots, Cambridgeshire: A & C Black, 2001.

Strunk and White, *Style Book.* 4th Ed., London, UK: Longman, 2000.

Zinsser, William. *Writing About Your Life.* New York: Marlowe & Co., 2004.

Zinsser, William. *On Writing Well.* New York: Collins, 2001.

Naomi Beth Wakan was born in London, England. She graduated with a degree in Social Work from Birmingham University, and shortly afterward emigrated to Canada and brought her family up in Toronto. Naomi worked as a psychotherapist specializing in early childhood traumas for several years before travelling extensively, including living two years in Japan.

She and her husband, Elias Wakan, moved to Gabriola Island in 1996 and opened Drumbeg House Studio, where Elias makes wood sculptures and Naomi paints, writes and does fabric art. Naomi has written educational books geared to children and many books for the adult market. Her essays and poetry have appeared in *Resurgence, Geist, Room of One's Own, Kansai Time Out, Far East Journal,* in many other magazines and on several websites. She has read her writings on CBC and in poetry venues. She is also a member of Gabriola Fibre Artists. *Segues,* a book of her poetry was published by Wolsak and Wynn Publishers in Spring, 2005.

MEMBER OF SCABRINI GROUP

Québec, Canada

2006